Acclaim for Judith Wills

The New Home Larder

'A well stocked larder is a cook's best friend, and Judith Wills's new book tells you everything you need to know about how to have one. *The New Home Larder* is sensible, down-to-earth, and remarkably comprehensive in scope. And the recipes are enticing. This book deserves a place in every kitchen library.'
Richard Ehrlich, author of *The Green Kitchen*

'Judith manages to make the boring task of stocking a larder a far more interesting prospect, with practical tips and delicious, yet easy recipes. As always with her books, I feel inspired enough to follow her advice!'
Joy Skipper, author and member of the Guild of Food Writers

'Having a well stocked store cupboard means you can, at a moment's notice, rustle something up for the family that's both nutritious and inexpensive. Judith has stacks of good ideas and delicious recipes to inspire you.'
Cathy Court, Co-founder and Director, netmums.com

'A fun, practical guide which imparts much-needed information.' *Bookseller*

The Green Food Bible

'*The Green Food Bible* covers vast areas of ground with balanced evaluations of some complicated subjects.' *The Times*

'Get to the heart of ethical eating with *The Green Food Bible*, which cuts through the labyrinth of ethical jargon on food and delivers the straight facts. Find out where to buy key organic foods, whether they really are ethical, and get great recipe ideas too.' *Marie Claire*

'A comprehensive and user-friendly guide to ethical and green eating... *The Green Food Bible* provides a wealth of information and easy to follow guidance... This beautifully illustrated book is packed with fascinating information.' *Green Living*

Judith Wills has written more best-selling food and healthy lifestyle titles than any other British author, and is translated into more than twenty languages. Her books have sold over two million copies worldwide and have appeared in the bestseller lists across the world. Her international bestseller *The Food Bible* has sold over 275,000 copies and was recently revised for its third edition. Her other books include *The Green Food Bible, The Children's Food Bible, The Diet Bible, Slim and Healthy Mediterranean, Slim and Healthy Vegetarian* and *Feeding Kids*, which she wrote with the Netmums organization.

Judith has made many television appearances and is an accomplished radio broadcaster. She writes for national newspapers and magazines, including the *Daily Mail, Mail on Sunday, Express, Sunday Times, Good Housekeeping, Woman's Weekly, Prima, Zest, Marie Claire, Waitrose Food Illustrated*, and *Saga* magazine. She also writes under the name the 'Diet Detective' for several magazines and websites, including 'ivillage' and 'saga' (www.dietdetective.net).

Judith holds talks and lectures at food fairs, literary festivals, on cruises and at the Eden Project in Cornwall. She is a long-standing member of the Guild of Food Writers and was a judge for the 2006 and 2008 GFW Book Awards.

Married with two grown-up sons, Judith lives on the borders of Herefordshire and Wales, where she cultivates an organic fruit and vegetable garden, greenhouse and orchard. She is also lucky enough to have a large, much-loved and much-used larder.

THE NEW HOME LARDER

JUDITH WILLS

eden project books

TRANSWORLD PUBLISHERS
61–63 Uxbridge Road, London W5 5SA
A Random House Group Company
www.rbooks.co.uk

First published in Great Britain
in 2009 by Eden Project Books
an imprint of Transworld Publishers

A CIP catalogue record for this book
is available from the British Library.

ISBN 9781905811311

All images courtesy of Shutterstock

Th... ...not,
l... ...ut,
c... ...hat
ir... ...on,

Address ... le the UK

The Random House Group Limited supports The Forest Stewardship
Council (FSC), the leading international forest-certification organization. All our
titles that are printed on Greenpeace-approved FSC-certified paper carry the FSC logo.
Our paper procurement policy can be found at
www.rbooks.co.uk/environment

Design www.andreanelli.com
Printed and bound in Great Britain by
Butler Tanner & Dennis Ltd, Frome

2 4 6 8 10 9 7 5 3 1

CONTENTS

Introduction

As a keen home cook who is lucky enough not only to have plenty of kitchen cupboards but also a much-loved larder, I cannot begin to explain how much I have enjoyed researching this book and how much pleasure I've gained from keeping good food stores and once again using them properly (after what I will admit has been a lapse of some years when the fridge, the freezer and 'using only fresh ingredients' took unreasonable precedence over the dusty shelves of the pantry).

But it's not just me. I've been aware for some time of a crusade – a growing feeling – that it is time to come back to many of the traditional food ideas and habits of our parents and grandparents. It's modern to be traditional! And a 'return to the larder' is an important part of this awareness.

Rightly, the larder is the cornerstone of the traditional kitchen and the 'main back-up troops' of the traditional cook. And that is why a new look at this long-neglected area of the kitchen and home is, I hope, very timely.

The idea of a well-stocked larder, and of being able to create delicious meals from our food stores even if there hasn't been the opportunity to go shopping, is extremely seductive. But few of us feel that our own kitchen stores measure up – we need help, both in planning and buying and in using what is in the larder for all kinds of meals. Many of us would also like to try making our own preserves, flavoured oils and so on for the first time.

Cooking from the larder also has many advantages other than practicality and pleasure. It has a green element, a health element and a wholesome concept – real cooking, using items carefully and often seasonally chosen, which can be bought or produced, stored and used for healthy, great-tasting meals without recourse to the fridge or freezer.

What I also intend to show you is exactly what we've been missing in terms of convenience. Our larders and storecupboards are a much neglected source of convenience food, comfort food, fast food, feast food and, often, inexpensive food. They are also endlessly versatile. From low-cost pulses and grains to top-of-the-range olive and seed oils and aged vinegars – your larder really can be your best friend when it comes to preparing snacks and meals, for one or for a whole family. Storecupboard ingredients also represent a huge range of cuisines across the world, so whatever your preferences, your style of cooking or your lifestyle, a well-stocked larder is a complete boon.

I've included in this book recipes that use a high proportion of storecupboard ingredients. With each, I have listed the fresh ingredients they contain so that you can see quickly whether or not you can cook this or that recipe today without going to the shops. I have also included a high percentage of recipes that use only one or two fresh items, and several in here use none at all.

While the accent is on convenience and practicality, I do hope that you'll also find plenty in here that is inspirational, and evocative both of times past and of future pleasures.

Judith Wills

PART 1 Your Larder

1 A New Look at Your Larder

In recent years the larder has come to be thought of as something we open when we want a jar of Marmite or tomato pasta sauce, or are looking for the soya sauce or cooking oil, and that's about it. Yes, there are cans inside that were bought years ago, but their age often tells their own story. For most of us, the idea of keeping a versatile larder has given way to using the freezer, the fridge or takeaway foods.

But now we have:

- The Slow Food movement.
- The growth of allotments and the increase in vegetable-growing.
- The green food movement and an awareness of the need to conserve energy.
- Prices of most basic foods higher than they have been for many years and thus, for a lot of us, a keen interest in keeping costs down where and when we can.
- A new interest in cooking with wholesome, indigenous ingredients and using seasonal recipes.
- A returning interest in the traditional methods of food preservation, such as bottling and preserves.
- Importantly, we also have a growing interest in quality foods that fit easily into our modern lifestyles.

So how does the larder, the storecupboard, fit in with all that? Well, very well . . .

With more emphasis on seasonal foods, on sourcing locally, on saving energy, and on home cooking, the larder is experiencing a real renaissance. The new home larder can become – should become – the most important area of your kitchen. Our grannies bought fresh and local when they could, but certainly didn't do so every day. What a pity that we've forgotten how to stock the larder and use it well!

You don't need a huge amount of space. I aim to show you how to stock your larder with products that really will get used within a few months, which will make your shopping, meal-planning and cooking life much easier and more enjoyable.

With a good storecupboard you need rely less on high-energy freezers and fridges and can save time and petrol on shopping. Less reliance on chilled and frozen foods will also mean that you may eat less meat and dairy produce – which is good for both the environment and your health.

Good use of the larder can also mean that you spend less on everyday items (essentials) and luxuries. And if you're saving money, you needn't feel guilty for occasionally stocking up with more luxurious items, or with some well-chosen ethnic items which aren't cheap but can make a great deal of difference to the taste and interest in meals made totally, or mainly, from the larder.

A well-planned larder means that you always have a quick and/or easy and delicious meal within sight – add just one or two fresh ingredients (even that is often unnecessary) and off you go. The possibilities are, literally, almost endless.

WHY THE LARDER IS IMPORTANT

It can save you so much time during a busy week (or life!) – you don't need to go shopping every day.

It also saves energy, both in petrol travelling to the shops and in freezer and fridge usage, thus it is a green option.

It can be relied on to help you produce any type of meal or snack, whether for one or for a whole family, easily and quickly.

It is healthy. Storecupboard cooking encourages us to make the most of healthy foods such as pulses and grains, and olive oil, rather than items such as meat and dairy produce, which need chilling. Later on (page 90) we will look at the health benefits of typical larder foods.

It can always help you turn something plain (e.g. an omelette or a salad) into something wonderful, interesting and tasty.

Saving money

Here are some of the ways you can save money with a good larder:

- I calculate that making your own preserves from your own produce saves about 80–90 per cent of the cost of bought versions, and that making your own using bought produce saves about 50 per cent. (These figures will, of course, vary, depending on factors such as whether or not you use seasonal produce and how many items you produce – in general, the more in a batch, the lower the price works out per item.)

- Because the shelf-life of most larder products is much longer than items you buy for the fridge (and, often, for the freezer), there is less likelihood of wastage through foods going off or becoming out of date. This also means that you can stock up the larder when you see items on special offer or similar (or perhaps share bulk-buys with neighbours) and thus reduce costs even more.

- Many of the storecupboard items you will buy are less expensive than fresh, chilled or frozen items of a similar nutritional value. For example, lentils and beef both contain protein, iron, B vitamins and energy (as well as other nutrients), but in a '£ per lb' comparison, lentils are approximately 80 per cent cheaper than beef.

Stocking your larder and creating a positive larder environment

Think about your lifestyle and what items will be of most use to you. Do you want a home delicatessen or a large supply of quick-cook pasta, or both?

Asking yourself a few questions about how you eat, your lifestyle and what you enjoy eating may help you plan out your larder shopping to maximum advantage.

For example:

- Think about how many people are in your household and will be using the larder. If you live alone you are more likely to need plenty of small packets and jars – once opened, many containers need to be used up quite quickly. For a large family the larger packs will be much more economical.

- Do you have lots of occasions when you need a fast meal? If so, you will need to stock up with plenty of quick-cook items such as pasta or couscous, and no-cook items such as tinned fish and jars of cheese.

- Do you have many times when people drop round for supper with little warning? In that case you might make sure your larder contains a few quick-to-prepare luxury items so that you can rustle up a delicious meal for a few people more or less from what you have in the cupboard. For example, that might be a table of meze-type dishes, including gourmet roast vegetables (aubergine, artichoke) in oil, feta cheese and olives, pasta salad with tomatoes in oil and olive pesto added to the dressing...

- Are you often just too tired or busy to cook? In that case, make sure the shelves are filled with items that you can eat more or less as they are – good-quality seafood and tuna, cooked pulses, and a selection of top-quality nuts such as walnuts and Brazils will offer quick and nutritious appetite soothers.

FRESH VERSUS STORED

People sometimes say to me that a meal or snack can't be healthy if you're just eating out of the larder. 'What about vitamin C?' 'What about all the chemicals that leach into food if it's canned?' 'What about the nutrients that are lost when things are heated to make them longlife?'

Well, the truth is that just because a food isn't fresh doesn't necessarily mean that it isn't healthy, or that it isn't something good – or even great – to eat. If these are your concerns, see what I have to tell you on page 90 about health issues and throughout the rest of this chapter and the A–Z for quality issues. Then try some of the recipes in the book and make up your own mind!

Flavour, taste and interest in your storecupboard

The reason so many people open their kitchen food cupboard, look at what's inside and then shut the door again is that the contents don't look appealing, they don't excite the tastebuds or any other senses and often don't, on short inspection, offer a glimpse of what fabulous meal or snack you might create from the selection you see.

That is because the shelves contain so many things that were bought on a whim and are now way out of date. In the shop, you looked and saw something great – but now you see only boredom.

However worthy or actually edible the contents are, they won't get out of that cupboard unless you feel good about what you see inside. What you need to do is re-create the mood you felt in the shop every time you look in the larder for something good to eat.

You need to be able to imagine interesting flavours, see colours good enough to eat and packaging or containers that tempt you to open them; catch fantastic aromas in your imagination and be fired with enthusiasm to make a meal from what you see.

Here are my tips for creating that blend:

Colour: Glass containers so you can see what's inside (but not suitable for herbs). Cellophane also lets you see through to what's there.

Individuality: You can create this by transferring shop-bought items to your own containers, such as enamel tins, china and glass jars, bottles and so on. Also by making your own unique storecupboard items such as jam, marmalade and flavoured oils.

Wholesomeness: Environmentally friendly packaging, and packaging that matches the contents. For example, bread flour in a box that looks as if it has been produced with care.

Cleanliness: If the shelves have drifts of old flour or ring-marks from leaking salad-dressing bottles or sauces, you won't feel positive about your larder. Keep it clean! (See page 85.)

Order: As with cleanliness, if you don't keep your shelves orderly so that you know where to find things, you're less likely to look (see page 88 for larder practicalities). In general, your larder will also look more inviting if you keep the more brightly coloured items to the front, and have each shelf contain one particular type of food (e.g. top shelf for all grains and pulses, bottom shelf for all sauces). This also helps with planning your restocking.

Novelty: Unusual packaging. Some new items you've never tried before (best bought in small quantities in case you decide you don't like them). Plenty of spices from around the world.

Luxury: Always keep a few luxury items to hand. You don't want a whole larder full of tins of Beluga caviar or truffle oil, but a few well-chosen 'treats' can be invaluable – perhaps used in minute amounts to liven up an otherwise mundane dish or used as a splash-out when a friend drops by unexpectedly or when you feel like something extravagant to cheer yourself up. Luxury items can often (but not always) provide a taste or visual kick that you may not get from lower-priced foods and condiments.

Quality: This doesn't necessarily equate to cost. There are more good-quality low-cost products than you may think, while often expensive cans and jars, etc., are of poor quality and hence poor value for money.

You need to shop with care and buy good quality when you can. In general, it is true that there are certain types of food which lend themselves very well to being in the storecupboard in cans, jars and so on (mustard, oils, preserves and sugars are obvious examples), while others (perhaps including canned fruits, bottled vegetables and juices in longlife cartons) may be hard to equate with true quality. Which cans cut the mustard? Which ready-made sauces, pastes and so on are good to buy and which aren't? This is stuff you need to know. You'll find more information on the tricky subject of quality within the individual food sections in Chapter 2, and the A–Z (pages 229–49) will be your best friend when shopping for the storecupboard as it contains my recommendations for products, brands and where to buy.

To recap . . .

A good larder is one that contains:

- Plenty of everyday items that you can use for quick meals, easy meals and emergencies (e.g. grains, pulses).

- Items that can boost the interest and taste of your meals (ethnic sauces, seasonings).

- Luxuries – things like top-notch canned fishes or vegetables.

- And lastly – things you have made yourself, such as relishes, preserves and pickles.

In the next chapter, we'll be looking at the perfect larder contents in more detail.

2 DOWN TO DETAIL

Now let us take a close look at the larder and the different types of food that should be in it, along with my quick tips and ideas on how they might be used in your menus and meals. I have also included some nutrition or historical notes where I felt they would be of interest.

For ease, I divide the contents of the larder into the different major food groups. Bear in mind, of course, that this isn't a definitive list, and it isn't intended to imply that everyone will need to stock up with everything here. Far from it — most of our larders are not large enough to do that. These are simply fairly comprehensive suggestions to get you thinking and list-writing, and hopefully to get you looking for, and trying, items you may have overlooked before.

For more detailed information on varieties, for my recommendations for actual brands and individual products, and where to purchase them, turn to the A–Z (pages 229–49).

Carbohydrates

Grains

Grains (the seeds of a variety of grasses and grass-like plants) are the main staple food across the world, rich in carbohydrates and starch and high in energy. Each world region has traditionally had its own staple grain (e.g. wheat in the UK, rice in India and corn in America), but today, certainly in the UK, we enjoy sampling all kinds of grains and a wide variety can be found even in basic supermarkets.

Most grains are farmed – i.e. grown commercially for sale – and these may have been developed over the years, improving upon the original, wild version. But you can also still find 'wild' grains here and there. Wild rice (a black grain which isn't in fact rice at all but a seed from a completely different plant) is one of the best known.

When you buy grains it helps if you know the terms relating to them, so here's a rundown (the words in brackets are other terms that may be used for the same thing). A well-stocked larder will probably contain a selection of these different grades of grain.

Whole grains (berries, groats, brown): Grains which are stripped from the plant and have no part of the berry removed, with the exception perhaps of a few inedible outer layers of hull. These are the most nutritious form of grain, as they retain the outer bran layers and the kernel where most of the nutrients lie. Whole grains in general take longer to cook than refined grains and have a chewier texture. Whole grains can be used cooked 'as is' in pilafs, salads and so on. Processed whole grains (e.g. rolled, cracked or milled) are quicker to cook and can be used in a variety of ways, such as in breakfast dishes.

Pearled grains (polished, white): These are more processed than whole grains, the layers of husk being removed to produce a grain that is quicker to cook and more tender to eat. Their nutrient levels are fairly seriously depleted (for example they have far fewer B-group vitamins and less magnesium), as is their fibre content. They can be used in both savoury and sweet dishes.

Cracked grains (grits): Processed grains that have been cut into small pieces so that they cook more quickly. They include couscous and bulghar wheat.

Rolled grains (flakes): The grains (usually whole grains) are steamed, rolled and flaked. There can be different degrees of rolling, so you may find 'fine', 'coarse' or 'whole' flakes (as in porridge oats). These have slightly fewer nutrients than unprocessed whole grains due to the steaming and rolling process which creates heat, but whole flakes will tend to be more nutritious than fine flakes. They are generally quick to cook and can be used for a variety of purposes, including in breakfast gruels, mueslis or granolas, and in baking cakes and biscuits.

Meal: Grains ground using a variety of techniques (traditionally stone-grinding, which retains the most nutrients, but roller techniques are now most often used) to a course or fine sand consistency (e.g. cornmeal/polenta). Meal is usually cooked with liquid to produce a soft cereal breakfast or savoury accompaniment, or to make rustic breads.

Flour: Finely ground grain (though sometimes flours can be made using pulses or even nuts, potatoes or other vegetables) which is used in breads, cakes, etc., and as a thickener for liquids or as coatings for fish and a variety of fried or baked foods. Flours can be stone-ground (see *Meal*, above) but most are milled by modern heat-inducing roller techniques, when the grain is rolled then sifted to make white flour. For wholemeal flour, the separated husk and residue from the rolling process is returned to the meal. Other flours are made using variants of this basic technique (see boxes, pages 30–1).

Bran: The outer husk of the grain, which is high in dietary fibre but is removed in milling pearl (white) grains. Bran can be found sold separately as an aid to the digestive system, but raw bran can interfere with the body's absorption of various nutrients and in my opinion is best avoided as a supplement.

Germ: The tiny embryo at the centre of the grain which contains high levels of certain nutrients (e.g. vitamin E) and high concentrations of unsaturated oils and protein. White flour has often had the germ removed, as the oil content tends to shorten its shelf-life, but wheatgerm can be bought as a food supplement to sprinkle on cereals, soups, salads and fruit, etc., and you can buy speciality wheatgerm breads.

Individual grains and their uses

WHEAT

Wheat is the most common bread flour as it is high in gluten, a protein which helps bread to rise and also gives wheat flour its gluey texture. Wheat flakes can also be used to make pasta or noodles (see *Pasta*, pages 32–3), in breakfast cereals and is the basis of most cakes, crackers, biscuits and pastries for sale in the UK. Whole wheat is a good source of fibre, B vitamins, magnesium and selenium. Refined wheat is a poor natural source of nutrients.

Bulghar wheat: Made from whole wheat, which is pre-soaked, then pre-cooked, and finally coarse ground and dried to speed up cooking time, as only reconstituting in boiling water is needed. Bulghar originates from the Middle East and is the basis of the salad tabbouleh and of Turkish pilafs. Bulghar wheat 'grains' can be processed into different sizes.

Couscous: Made from hard flour (usually durum wheat flour) which is traditionally spread out, sprinkled with water and formed into tiny balls. Almost all the couscous you will find for sale in the UK is pre-cooked by steaming and then dried so that you simply soak it in boiling water to use it. Couscous makes a good substitute for bulghar wheat, rice or especially pasta, and goes well with most traditional Mediterranean and North African dishes.

Cracked wheat: Simply cracked wholewheat kernels (unlike bulghar, not pre-cooked), thus it takes less time to cook than wholewheat berries.

RICE

Rice is the world's most consumed grain, leading wheat by a small margin. All rice is gluten-free and is one of the foods known to have a low risk of intolerance. While most rice is simply cooked and eaten as it is, boiled, steamed or fried, it can also be turned into noodles or flour, rice cakes, rice wine (sake) and so on.

Brown rice: Wholegrain rice, with a nutty flavour and slightly chewy texture. It is a good source of B vitamins and magnesium and is high in dietary fibre.

White rice: The polished grain with the outer husk removed and containing few nutrients. White rice is classified mostly by the size of the grain.

Long-grain rice: The long, slender grains stay separate and fluffy after cooking, so this is the best choice if you want to serve rice as a side dish, or as a bed for sauces. Basmati rice from India is one of the better known luxury long-grain rices.

Partially cooked long-grain rices: There are many brands of long-grain rice which help speed up cooking times. These easy-cook rices are white and are partially cooked after milling and then dried to reduce cooking time to around 10 minutes.

Pre-cooked long-grain rice: As opposed to easy-cook rice, this is cooked before milling, resulting in grains that stay separate when cooked but need as long a cooking time as ordinary white rice, or even longer. In my opinion the texture can be tough and the taste disappointing. Pre-cooked rices usually come in boxes with words such as 'fluffy rice' or 'separate grains every time'. I wouldn't bother with them if I were you, as it is so easy to cook decent basmati or other long-grain rice properly once you know how.

Medium-grain rice: Shorter and plumper than long-grain. Traditional risotto rice (such as the well-known arborio) is a medium-grain rice. It can also be used for paella (or you can find traditional Spanish rices for paella-cooking) and other fried and baked savoury rice dishes.

Short-grain rice: Almost round, with moist grains that stick together when cooked. It's the best choice for rice pudding.

Sticky rice (glutinous rice, sushi rice): The short-grain rice of Japan and the right type to use for sushi and rice balls, as it holds well together and is also easier to eat with chopsticks. In fact it contains no gluten (in common with all rice) and so the 'glutinous' tag is a misnomer.

Jasmine rice: Common in Thailand, this has a faint aroma and is a slightly sticky long-grain rice.

Red rice: The best type comes from the Camargue region of France, although you can also get red rices from other areas. It's a wholegrain, short-grain rice with a good, strong, nutty flavour and firm texture. Good hot or cold and makes a great salad.

Wild rice: Blackish in colour, with very thin grains which take a long time to cook compared with other rices. Often used mixed with long-grain rice.

Almost-instant partially cooked rices: There is a growing band of rice pouches containing virtually cooked rice (mostly long-grain white, but also brown and some flavoured varieties) which will finish cooking in around 2 minutes in a microwave oven. These types are handy for emergencies but tend to be lacking in the texture department – they are often slightly tough. My own tip is to add 2 tbsps water to the pouches and increase the heating time to double what the packet says, while reducing the power level from high to medium-high. Then leave to stand for at least 3–4 minutes and fluff up with a fork.

OATS

Oats are rich in soluble fibre, which helps to fight high levels of LDL cholesterol in the blood. Because they are, for grains, relatively high in fat and protein, they are also low on the glycaemic index, which means they are better at keeping hunger at bay than many other grains, and they have a pleasant, nutty flavour. The high oil content means that oats can go rancid if kept too long.

While most of us only get our oats via porridge or muesli, they are also a good addition to bread, biscuits and crumble toppings, and are, of course, a main ingredient of flapjacks. Scotland, with the cool, moist climate that oats prefer, is famous for oat-growing, but they have also been grown throughout the rest of Europe as food for mankind since the days of Christ and are now grown in most areas of the world.

Traditional porridge oats (rolled oats): These are just lightly rolled to flatten them, while instant porridge oats are pre-cooked and just need adding to hot liquid for a breakfast cereal.

Groats: The whole oat berry, which has simply been minimally processed to remove its outer hull. Groats need to be soaked and cooked for a long time to become edible.

Pinhead oats: Groats (see above) that have been chopped small. They take longer to cook than rolled oats or flakes but less time than the whole groats. They can be used for porridge.

Oatmeal: Dried and then milled and/or sieved oats of different-sized particles, depending on the grade, which can be used to coat foods before frying (herrings being a typical example) or added to burgers to bulk out meat. It can also be used to eke out wheat flour in many recipes. Pinhead oats (see above) are coarse, 'rough' are medium and 'superfine' are the finest. Oatmeal is a traditional ingredient of the easy Scottish dessert Athol Brose – a mix of thick cream, whisky, honey and oatmeal.

RYE

A staple of northern European cuisine as it is hardy enough to grow in cold areas. It is made into a heavy bread or crackers. Rye berries are soaked and cooked as for wheat berries, while rolled rye flakes are often among the ingredients of mueslis. Breads made from rye have a lower glycaemic index than wheat breads and thus have a better long-term satiety value.

BARLEY

The earliest-known cultivated cereal, barley has become less popular in recent times. A pity, as the grain is highly nutritious with excellent amounts of minerals, including zinc and iron, B vitamins and fibre. Its high soluble fibre content makes it a good choice for people with high cholesterol.

Pot barley (Scotch barley): The most nutritious form of barley you're likely to find in most UK outlets. It has the outer husk removed. It needs 8 hours' soaking, then about 2 hours' cooking and can be used like wheat or rye berries in stews and soups, or in pilafs or as a rice substitute.

Pearl barley: This has the outer husk, bran and germ removed, leaving just the endosperm. This is then steamed, rounded and polished, and so is much less nutritious. Its main purpose is to thicken soups and stews and to add starch. It will cook in around half an hour.

Barley flakes: Like wheat, oat and rye flakes, these can be used in muesli – they are part-cooked pot barley which has been rolled and dried.

CORN (MAIZE)

The tall-growing leafy plants of corn – or maize – are indigenous to the Americas but can be found in many areas of the world, including the UK. A good source of carotenes and folate, corn cobs are more usually eaten in the UK as a vegetable, either whole or as frozen or canned kernels (see *Vegetables*, page 54), but the grain can be dried and used as popcorn, ground into cornflour (see box, page 31) or ground into polenta, a type of cornmeal. Polenta is a popular starchy food in northern Italy. Traditionally the corn was stone-ground into the texture of a coarse or fine sand, then stirred in a pan with boiling water and salt for around 40 minutes to form a soft, rich purée served with savoury dishes. Traditional polenta meal can be found in some shops, but much of the polenta meal sold in the UK today is the easy-cook kind. This has been pre-cooked, dried and then re-milled into fine particles which are quick to cook in a pan with water, usually with the addition of butter and/or cheese for a less bland flavour. Polenta can be served as a 'wet' side dish or allowed to cool and firm up, then sliced and grilled or fried.

BUCKWHEAT

Buckwheat is not an actual grain but the seed of a plant related to rhubarb. The triangular seeds, husked, are traditionally used as a grain in countries such as Russia and Poland. One of the most popular dishes is kasha, a simple, toasted

buckwheat side dish or salad which brings out a good nutty flavour in the seeds.

Buckwheat can also be ground into flour which is used for a variety of things, including Russian blinis (pancakes), flatbreads or soba noodles. Ground buckwheat can be used as a breakfast cereal, cooked like porridge.

You will find both toasted and untoasted buckwheat seeds for sale in the UK. You may find toasted buckwheat sold as 'kasha'.

WHEAT FLOUR TYPES

White flour: Highly-refined wheat flour naturally contains few nutrients, but in the UK it is fortified by law with added calcium (the exception being some self-raising varieties), iron and some B vitamins. Flour can be whitened naturally by storing it for a few weeks (unbleached flour), but it is also bleached artificially in industrial manufacturing processes.

Plain flour: White flour may be plain flour, which is a multipurpose type, usually a blend of 'hard' and 'soft' flours, and, indeed, in the USA it is called multipurpose flour. It is used in baking cakes, biscuits, desserts, etc.

Strong flour: A white flour made from 'hard' wheat with a high gluten and protein content which produces the best bread. Durum wheat is a hard wheat which is made into strong durum flour ideal for pasta-making.

Brown flour: Contains 85 per cent of the whole grain and therefore more of the bran than white flour, and so is a 'halfway house' between white and wholemeal or wholegrain flour. Brown flour in the UK is fortified by law with added calcium, iron and some B vitamins.

Granary flour: A mixture of wholemeal, rye and white flours with added malted whole grains.

Wholemeal flour (wholewheat flour): Flour milled from the whole grain of the wheat. The term 'wholemeal' could also refer to flours milled from the whole grain of other types of grain (e.g. oats, rye), but it normally refers to wheat.

Self-raising flour: The raising agent bicarbonate of soda is added to plain white flour so that in recipes where rising is required (e.g. cakes, soufflés) there is no need to add baking powder.

Semolina flour: A coarse-ground meal made using the endosperm of the durum wheat grain. It is used for making pasta and hard Mediterranean-style breads.

Sauce flour: This very finely milled flour is sold in small boxes which can be used to make sauces such as béchamel (savoury white sauce) without the need for added fat. Or it can be used in the normal sauce recipes when it is less likely to go 'lumpy' and produces a silky-textured result.

QUINOA

This ancient, small seed was a staple of the Incas. It is quick to cook, has a mild flavour similar to couscous and a slightly crunchy texture, and comes in several colours, from white or pink through to red and black. Higher in protein than cereals such as wheat or oats, and rich in iron and zinc, it can be steamed for around 15 minutes as a side dish or as a substitute for rice or pasta, or added to soups and stews. Steamed, rolled and flaked quinoa can be used instead of oatmeal to make a hot cereal.

SPELT

Spelt is believed to be the ancient ancestor of wheat and it has a similar taste, though it is perhaps a little more intense. It contains more fibre, more protein and a little more fat than modern wheat. Though it does contain gluten, it seems to be tolerated better than wheat by many people. It can be used in any recipe as a substitute for wheat berries, flakes or flour, but in bread-making proving time may be reduced, so watch carefully to make sure that the rise doesn't collapse. This eagerness to rise means that spelt is a particularly good flour to use for quick bread-making when the dough is left to rise just once.

OTHER TYPES OF FLOUR

Cornflour: A light, fine flour ideal for thickening casseroles, gravies and for sauce-making.

Arrowroot: A flour useful for thickening dessert dishes such as fruit compotes and fruit fillings for pies and patisserie, as it goes transparent when blended with hot liquid.

Gluten-free flours: For people who are allergic to gluten (found in wheat, rye, barley and oats) there are several other grain flours that can be used to replace these, including corn flour, rice flour and buckwheat flour. Special gluten-free bread-making flours are available which contain forms of added protein to help make bread rise.

Non-grain flours: Flours made from potatoes and pulses are widely available these days. They are also free from gluten. Soya flour is particularly nutritious and high in protein, while another common pulse flour is made from chickpeas. These flours are often mixed with other flours and used for breads, baking and all types of savoury and sweet dishes.

Nut flours: Ground nuts (e.g. chestnuts or blanched almonds) are sometimes described as 'nut flours', but these are not really suitable to use as a straight replacement for grain flours other than in small amounts (for instance, in a fruit crumble topping a small amount of nut flour can be used instead of some of the wheat flour), as their composition, including a high fat content, is so different.

MILLET

If you ever had a budgie you'll know what unhulled millet looks like, but it's a perfectly good food for humans too. This grass seed, which has long been used in Africa and Asia, is not as rich in minerals as some of the other grains described above, but it is a reasonable source of protein and folate and is gluten-free. It is often toasted, which improves the flavour. Use it instead of couscous or as a soup and stew thickener, or make it into flatbread.

TEFF

This tiny seed from Africa is the world's smallest grain and is sold unrefined. It is rich in protein and calcium, and is gluten-free. It has a sweetish flavour and comes in different colours, from cream to terracotta. Use it instead of quinoa (see page 31) or cook it like porridge for breakfast.

Pasta and noodles

Pasta

Dried pasta is surely the most useful of all storecupboard items, with much to recommend it and little to get sniffy about. It stores easily, lasts almost for ever without spoiling, cooks quickly, comes in a myriad of different shapes, sizes and colours so that one need never get bored, is comfort food, and is bland enough to adapt to hundreds of different uses while still being tasty enough to be enjoyable for its own sake. It is also a healthy enough item – and if you choose wholemeal versions it is more than healthy enough, being a great source of dietary fibre, magnesium and B vitamins. And with a fairly low glycaemic index count (whether you choose white or whole), it can also be a good food for slimmers and diabetics.

For pasta salads: penne, macaroni, fusilli, conchiglie.

To go in soups: orzo, orecchiette, tubettini, conchiglette.

To go with chunky sauce: pappardelle, fettuccine, fusilli, farfalle, ziti, conchiglie.

To go in casseroles: macaroni, penne, rigatoni, fusilli.

To go with creamy sauce: fettuccine, spaghetti, penne, tagliatelle.

For stuffing and baking: cannelloni, lasagne, tufoli.

People with a wheat allergy can, instead, buy pasta and noodles made from other grains, such as rice, corn, quinoa or buckwheat (see A–Z for brands and stockists).

People with an egg allergy can eat dried pasta, as most of it is made simply from flour and water (check the label, though, as a few makes do contain egg), unlike fresh pasta which is made with eggs.

While you don't need a hundred different types of pasta in the cupboard, in the box above are a few ideas for a selection that will ensure you have the right shape for whatever dish you intend to prepare. The Italians tend to pride themselves on serving the 'right' pasta with the right sauce – for example, a chunky sauce should be served with pasta that will hold it well, such as farfalle (bows) or conchiglie (shells).

And don't forget that pasta is a brilliant addition to many soups and even stews and casseroles. It helps to thicken the gravy, sauce or soup and also provides carbohydrate so you don't need to serve bread.

You should also consider stocking one or two packets of coloured pastas – a spinach pasta (pasta verde) looks very good with a creamy, pale-coloured sauce, for example, while children love tricolour pasta shapes. Black pasta is pasta flavoured with squid or cuttlefish ink, which is ideal served with shellfish. Other flavours include tomato, beetroot (pasta viola), carrot (pasta rossa), winter squash (pasta arancione), truffle (truffle pasta, or pasta al tartufo) and chilli.

Wholemeal pasta has a beautiful nutty flavour and a little goes a long way, so it is ideal filling food for hungry weight watchers. It usually needs a little longer cooking time than white pasta but, that said, the difference is minimal. Obviously, the thinner and smaller the pasta, the more quickly it will cook, so if you're really short of time choose small pastas such as spaghettini and vermicelli rather than rigatoni or penne.

Noodles

For Asian dishes you need egg-thread noodles (which come in various thicknesses and are wheat-based) and/or rice noodles. Soba noodles are useful for Japanese dishes and have a great taste.

Breads

While there is nothing that will keep in the larder that is an exact substitute for a loaf of good-quality fresh bread – nor indeed anything quite so evocative and delicious – there are some items that you might consider useful to have in store for those times when you forget to buy a loaf or the children empty the bread bin after school and forget to mention it!

A number of breads that can store for several weeks or so are also useful in their own right as traditional accompaniments to ethnic dishes, or as snacks or party foods.

Here are some of the breads and bread alternatives that can be purchased for the larder. Store them in dry, dark, cool conditions to maximize their useful life. And when buying, search for the packets with the 'best before' or 'use by' date as far ahead as possible.

Pittas: Both white and wholewheat often come in packets with a long shelf-life.

Chapatis and naans: A variety of flavours of these breads also come in packets which keep well for several weeks and are ideal as a quick carbohydrate to go with a curry.

Wraps/tortillas/flatbreads: Usually made from wheat flour, these can be bought in longlife packs containing several items. They make an ideal alternative to bread for a sandwich or can be part of a Mexican meal.

Rye bread: Dark, heavy and thinly sliced, German rye bread comes in longlife packets in several varieties (e.g. seeded or plain). This bread is nutritious and is good for open sandwiches or cut small for instant canapé bases; it is also good to slice and use with dips. It is less good for toasting.

French toasts: Crisp little slices of toasted bread sold in smallish packs. They aren't the tastiest of things, but are OK in an emergency for breakfast with marmalade or as canapés. You can also buy crisprolls – little baked crispy rolls – which are similarly useful.

Crackers and biscuits

It's useful to have a large, airtight box in the larder containing a selection of crackers and savoury and sweet biscuits. Some crackers are very high in salt, but there are some low-salt varieties available (see A–Z). Typical cheese biscuits can also be high in fat, while most sweet biscuits are high in both fat and sugar. Again, healthier options are available, and choosing wholegrain varieties will help boost their nutritional profile.

As a change from wheat-based biscuits, try those based on rye and oats. Both go particularly well with cheeses and hummus.

Once opened, even in an airtight tin crackers tend to soften and become stale quite quickly.

Crisps and snacks

While it may not be wise to have a larder stuffed full of crisps and the like because these snack foods tend to be quite high in salt and fat, they can make a delicious occasional treat and several brands have appeared over recent years which help you feel less guilty about eating them.

Alternatives to potato crisps are crisps made from other vegetables, such as parsnips or beetroot, and wheat-based snacks (but I have yet to discover one that I find anywhere near as enjoyable as good vegetable crisps). You can also buy broad-bean snacks which are healthy and tasty, if sometimes a bit too crunchy for my liking (see A–Z).

Then there's popcorn – the ready-made variety is usually thickly coated in sugar, honey or syrup, but it is easy to make your own. You can buy unpopped corn for popping and simply heat it in a heavy, lidded saucepan until it pops – or there are popcorn-makers available. Home-made popcorn can be flavoured with honey, herbs, spices or sea salt and makes a good, healthy snack.

Breadsticks are a good, low-fat, low-calorie option if you like to crunch without many calories, and they make a good vehicle for dips, but they contain little in the way of nutrients.

Sugars, syrups and honeys

Sugar

Sugar will store almost indefinitely if it's kept in dry conditions, so it's worth having a few different types in your larder. Yes, sugar is quite high in calories, and contains no or virtually no nutrients apart from carbohydrate for energy, but if you use small amounts wisely, for people in normal health it won't do you or your waistline any harm.

There's no real need to stock white sugar – which is highly refined – at all but here is a short guide to the different sugar types and what you may find them useful for:

White sugar: In the UK about half the white sugar sold is made from the sugar-beet crop in our fields. The beet is 'cooked' to extract the sweet juice, which then goes through several processes, including bleaching, to produce grains of sugar. Sugar from beet can be coloured with bought-in molasses in the factory to produce 'golden' or brown sugar, or Demerara sugar.

The most common type of white sugar is granulated, for everyday use. Caster sugar is simply a finer grade which dissolves more quickly and is useful for baking and meringues. Icing sugar is white sugar which has been powdered – as well as its obvious use for icings it is useful when you want to sweeten fruit purées and compotes, or anything where almost instant dissolving without much heat is an advantage. And there is also preserving sugar – large crystals suitable for jam-making, etc., as they give off less scum when boiled. You can also buy jam sugar with added pectin to help set fruits, such as strawberries, which have a low pectin content – but this isn't the same as preserving sugar.

Cane sugar: Most of the remainder of the sugar we eat is cane sugar – extracted from sugar-cane plants grown on plantations in countries such as Jamaica and Barbados. If the sugar you are buying is from cane rather than beet, this will almost always be printed on the label. Cane sugar can also become 'white sugar' through processing, but is often sold in the less processed forms described below.

Raw sugar: This is the crude, unrefined sugar sold in solid lumps with a strong flavour – you will find it in specialist shops, but rarely in the supermarket.

Muscavado (Barbados) sugar: This is partially refined, moist, soft sugar which contains some of the molasses from the cane. It is dark brown with a strong flavour ideal for rich fruit cakes and puddings.

Brown sugar: Other brown sugars suitable for cooking are simply labelled 'dark soft brown sugar' (more flavour) or 'light soft brown sugar' (less

flavour). These are moist, fine-grain sugars which tend to go lumpy in the cupboard over time, especially if exposed to the air.

Demerara sugar: Large, light-brown sugar crystals used mainly for coffee and in some recipes, it is made either from coloured sugar-beet crystals (see above) or from partly refined cane sugar.

Speciality sugars: You can find vanilla sugar (white caster sugar with added vanilla extract), but it is easy (and better) to make your own by adding a whole vanilla pod to your sugar in a jar and leaving it for the aromas to infuse. Palm sugar is made from neither beet nor cane but from the date-palm sap, and is widely used in Asian dishes. If you're a keen Asian chef you may like to stock some. Maple sugar is a sticky sugar refined from maple syrup.

Sugar cubes are simply crystallized white or brown sugar (either beet or cane) formed into cubes for coffee or tea, and you can also get extra large sugar crystals for tea and coffee, or stick crystals (sugar adhering to a small stick which you swizzle into your drink). I can't really see the point of any of these, especially if you're short of larder space.

Treacle and syrup

These are by-products from the sugar-refining process.

Molasses/treacle: Made from the syrup which is left behind as residue when sugar cane is processed. Light molasses come from a first boiling and medium molasses from a second, while darker molasses – black treacle, or blackstrap molasses, as it is known in the USA – come from a later boiling and has a 'burnt caramel', strong, slightly bitter flavour. The darker the molasses the stronger and more bitter edge it has. Some people buy black molasses for its said nutritional benefits – it contains some minerals such as calcium, iron and magnesium – but to be honest, unless you enjoy it, I'd rather get my minerals from other foods. The medium treacles are good used sparingly in rich desserts, dark cakes and savoury dishes, such as home-baked beans.

Golden syrup: Also refined from the residue syrup from the sugar-making process. While it is a 'light treacle', it uses a patented process which converts the sugar (sucrose) into fructose and glucose, which then goes through further blending to make a smooth, thick syrup that won't crystallize. It can be used in many baking recipes and desserts, or as a pour-over or on toast. It contains very small amounts of some nutrients, such as potassium.

Maple syrup: The syrup from the sap of the maple tree. It is very sweet and its clean vibrant taste is to my mind preferable to that of golden syrup. Its most famous use is with American pancakes and waffles. It is a good choice for vegans, who don't eat bee products, as a substitute for honey.

Corn syrup: This syrup (extracted from the corn grains) is popular in the USA and used instead of golden syrup or honey in desserts, baking, etc., but is not easy to come by in the UK. It has no nutritional benefits.

Honey

Honey is the sweet product made by bees from the nectar of flowers. Honey is mostly a mixture of sugar and water with a small amount of nutrients (but really too small to make much difference to your health in normal quantities).

The best honeys are those collected from bees who have eaten the nectar from a particular plant – the honey equivalent of a single-estate tea or wine, perhaps. These are always the most expensive. The flavour and colour of single-source honey depends upon the type of flower that the bees fed on to produce it. Stored in dark, dry conditions, honey will keep for a very long time, especially if it is unopened, so it pays to have two or three varieties to use depending on the purpose.

Pale, mild honeys: Including acacia and orange blossom, these are ideal used in hot lemon drinks or drizzled on to breakfast cereal, sponge cakes or yogurt.

Golden, stronger honeys: These, such as clover, are good all-purpose honeys, great on bread or yogurt or used in ice cream.

Dark, strong honeys: Examples are thyme and heather, which are excellent in robust desserts and stirred into savoury dishes requiring honey.

Manuka honey: Well known for its ability to act as an antibacterial, healing wounds. Although it does have a very strong flavour, it is delicious, if a bit of an acquired taste. Spread it thinly on toast or strong bread.

Honeycomb: The wax structure where the honey is originally found. This wax is perfectly edible and the honey it contains is delicious (varying again, on what the bees fed on) because it has been through no refining process.

Set honey: Made commercially by stirring runny honey until it becomes firm because crystals are formed. Runny or set is personal preference, but of course runny is preferable for pouring while set may be less messy for spreading. If runny honey turns crystallized in your cupboard, you can restore it to runniness by warming the jar gently in hot water.

Blended honey: This is the cheapest type you can buy. It may be a blend from several different countries. While the taste will usually be inferior to single-type honeys, it is perfectly good for use in baking and other cooked dishes. Indeed, top-quality honeys are wasted used in baking, as their particular characteristics tend to disappear when heated.

Protein foods

Fish

While nothing can quite replace fresh fish, tinned fish has its own – different – charm and uses. Forgetting white fish (which has never been successfully canned), there are plenty of oily fish and shellfish options that can be very useful storecupboard residents.

Salmon, tuna, herring, sardines, mackerel and pilchards, crab, prawns, crayfish, octopus and more – all come in a range of different qualities and types. You can get canned fish in a variety of media, too. Let's have a look at the health and flavour implications of the various options.

In oil: Much of the canned oily fish sold still comes in oil, which can vary from basic vegetable oil up to extra-virgin olive oil. This is one of the best media for oily fish and may help retain some of the omega-3 oils in the fish itself. It is, however, high in calories and the fish is best well drained and patted on kitchen paper before serving. Decent-quality oils will probably help the fish taste better than those canned in cheap blended oils. Sometimes you'll find herbs or other flavourings added to the oil, which, in my opinion, add little to the fish.

Shellfish is rarely canned in oil – being a low-fat product, it doesn't suit the oil-canned concept so well.

In brine: Tuna and other fish are often sold canned in brine. Slimmers may feel this is a better option than oil, but the resultant fish is high in salt, which may not be a good idea for people with high blood pressure, for example. We mostly do eat much more salt as a nation than we should, so it seems a bit crazy to buy fish in brine when you can almost always find a better option, which are:

In water: Tuna and other fish canned in water have little salt and are a healthy, low-fat option.

In tomato sauce: Robust fish such as mackerel, sardines and pilchards are often canned in a rich tomato sauce. This is a very healthy option – the tomatoes add important lycopene (a regular intake of which can help to prevent cancers) to your diet. Just as important, it is tasty and, heated through lightly, makes an ideal snack on wholewheat toast. Used cold it's a great lunchtime salad component, or the fish can be mashed with some of the sauce for a sandwich filling (use sturdy bread).

In vinegar: This could be OK if you like vinegar, but often the vinegars used aren't great, and the taste will mask the taste of the fish – which is often shellfish like cockles and mussels.

Other media: Sometimes you can find fish in a variety of special sauces, such as mustard and dill or curry, but none that I would rush to buy.

Omega-3 content of canned oily fish

Most people are now aware that we should eat 1–2 portions of oily fish a week. Canned oily fish, such as salmon, mackerel and sardines, makes a handy way of getting one or both of these portions. The omega-3 oils in these fish are retained quite well during the canning process, which involves heating the contents and the can.

But tests show that the omega-3 levels in tuna, whether it is canned in oil, brine or water, are so significantly reduced that there is hardly any left. So if you enjoy canned tuna, don't add it to your weekly oily fish tally.

Canned varieties

Now let's have a quick look at the different varieties of canned fish and how you might use them. Do bear in mind that it really is important to go for the best quality you can find (which will probably be reflected in the price) if you are going to be using the fish for anything other than a very basic sandwich, heavily disguised with mayonnaise or similar. The A–Z will give you more information about varieties.

Red salmon: Can be flaked into cooked pasta with a lemony yogurt or parsley and crème fraiche sauce and eaten hot.

Pink salmon: Flake into cooked rice with chopped vegetables and vinaigrette and serve as a salad.

Tuna: The Marine Conservation Society suggests avoiding bluefin and albacore, so go for yellowfin. Tuna goes well with a tomato sauce, stirred into pasta shapes or for sandwiches. A huge variety is now available, including ready-seared in a can

Herring rollmops: Douse in natural yogurt with chopped dill leaves stirred in.

Herring fillets: These are a good source of omega-3s and come in oil, or you can find it in sauces such as mustard or tomato.

Mackerel in oil: Can be whizzed in the blender with cream cheese to make a pâté or sandwich filling.

Mackerel or pilchards in tomato sauce: Mash for a sandwich filling or eat with some crisp salad leaves and cucumber. Mackerel also comes in other varieties, such as with peppercorns or mustard.

Sardines in oil: Do try to find good-sized ones, which can be drained, stuffed with sultanas and pine nuts with parsley and grilled to serve with crusty bread.

Let's look at some of my own favourite types of pulse and how you might cook and use them. For an overview, see the box on page 46.

Aduki beans: Small and red, they make a good purée and are great in salads.

Black beans: Widely used in the Caribbean and Latin America, and with a strong savoury flavour, they make good additions to soups and stews and can also make a good bean purée or dip with lemon juice.

Black-eyed beans (black-eyed peas): These medium-sized, pale beans with a black 'smudge' on the side are a popular ingredient in African and American cooking – good served with bacon or sausages or as 'peas and rice'. They need a fairly short soaking and cooking time.

Borlotti beans: Robust, mid-sized, pinkish-brown, pretty and nutty borlottis are great in meat casseroles and in any dish where you don't want the pulse to break up, as they tend to retain their shape well. They are also used in Italian cooking for bean and pasta soups and in minestrone.

Broad beans: While in the UK we pod and cook our broad beans when they are fresh, in other countries they are often dried and used like other pulses. They will turn brown with a meaty flavour and texture, and in Egypt and elsewhere they may be called fava beans. You can use them in casseroles and stews.

Butter beans (lima beans): Soft, large, flat, cream-coloured beans which have a very soft flesh and are excellent made into a purée as a change from hummus; lovely in a tomato, onion and tuna salad, and, crushed into a stew, can help to thicken it. They also make a good white bean soup and an excellent pâté.

Cannellini beans: A relative of the larger butter bean, these are smallish, oval beans which are a classic addition to a bean salad, Italian soups and stews, and can be puréed to serve with fish or poultry.

Chickpeas (garbanzo beans): The classic ingredient of Greek hummus, these peas look a little like shelled hazelnuts in shape and size. The round, yellowish beans sometimes have a fairly tough skin, which, while edible, you can remove by hand after cooking and before using – something I tend to do only when I am making a purée or dip. Chickpeas marry very well with stir-fried, grilled or roasted sweet peppers (much used in Spain) and are an excellent Indian curry ingredient, either with other vegetables or to eke out meat or poultry. Puréed, they are famous as chana dhal. In the Middle East they are often made into little balls and cooked to become delicious falafel patties – the veggie burger equivalent. They are rich in vitamin E

and soluble fibre, and are higher in polyunsaturated oils than some other beans.

Flageolet: A delicate, pale green French bean with a mild flavour – good in salads and also goes well with lamb.

Haricot beans: Baked beans in tomato sauce are usually the white haricot bean. Haricots can be used in meat or vegetable casseroles, winter soups or to make your own version of beans in tomato sauce.

Lentils: Lentils are the most popular dried pulse in the UK, probably because they are very versatile and quick to cook, needing no soaking or fast boiling. You can use these small, circular beans pre-cooked in a variety of dishes including salads, as an accompaniment to many items – especially good with salmon and other oily fish – and as the protein source in a curry. Lentils make an excellent winter soup – either puréed or left as they are – rich, deep-flavoured comfort food.

My favourite lentils are brown or the smaller, dark greeny-brown Puy lentils, which do have a slightly finer texture and flavour. Puy retain their shape well and make a particularly good salad dressed with vinaigrette, or a side dish. Green lentils are a good alternative to brown. Black lentils are not easy to find but make an interesting diversion from all the more usual types and can be used in all the same ways. Red and yellow lentils contain fewer nutrients than all the others as they have been skinned (and split). Their

Nuts and seeds

While we all have a packet of mixed chopped nuts in the kitchen cupboard, most of us tend to walk past the whole nut section in the supermarket, which is a great pity.

Few people realize that nuts – and seeds – are hugely beneficial health foods, as well as legitimate, extremely useful and delicious members of any larder. Nuts are seeds by another name – the fruit of trees, which can be eaten fresh off the tree or stored (given the right conditions) for weeks or even months.

Most nuts are high in 'good' unsaturated fats – often mono-unsaturated (like olive oil), but sometimes polyunsaturated (like sunflower and most other plant oils). This fat means that nuts are quite high in energy (calories) and I have often been told by people watching their weight that they won't eat nuts because they're 'fattening'.

In fact, nuts are very healthy, natural, nutrient-rich foods, very satisfying and useful, and ideal in any slimming or weight-maintenance diet. Most are high in protein and dietary fibre, and most contain very good amounts of vitamin E (not easy to come by in the typical modern Western diet) and B vitamins. Most are also high in a range of minerals, including iron, calcium (nuts are an important source of this mineral for vegans, and for vegetarians who don't want to eat too much dairy produce), magnesium, zinc and selenium (three minerals with antioxidant action and thus with a big role to play in helping to prevent ageing and illnesses such as cancer and arterial disease). Several trials have shown that nut-eating can reduce harmful blood-cholesterol levels, so anyone who needs to keep their cholesterol in check should eat nuts, not avoid them.

You only need a few, on a regular basis, to get all the benefits. Research shows that people who often eat nuts are half as likely to succumb to a heart attack as people who never eat them. As with any other food, it's all a matter of portion control and common sense.

NUT ALLERGIES

One word of caution: nuts are one of the most common causes of sensitivity or allergy, particularly peanuts, with about one in 200 people having a reaction. They can cause a serious instant reaction called anaphylactic shock. Walnuts, Brazils, cashews and sesame seeds are four other fairly common triggers.

A nut allergy tends to run in families and often starts in childhood. To help prevent this, peanuts and other nuts shouldn't be given to children under the age of one. For more information on food allergies visit www.allergyuk.org; tel. 01322 619898.

The best nuts and seeds for health are those which have received minimal processing – just picked or harvested (and maybe shelled), then stored in cool, dark, dry conditions before being sold to you, who should also store them in a similar way.

You can buy these 'basic' fresh (or as good as fresh) nuts in all supermarkets now, though you may get more choice in a specialist shop or even a health-food store (see A–Z). But you are much more likely to find a bigger section devoted to nuts which have been more highly processed – for example, salted nuts or toasted nuts. Adding salt to nuts turns them into a high-salt food – something we should try to avoid, especially if prone to high blood pressure or heart disease, while toasting or roasting nuts alters the composition of the unsaturated fats they contain and may make them much less healthy. So my advice is to store enough natural nuts in your larder, but go easy on the salted and roasted kind.

All this information also applies to seeds.

Nuts

Here is a rundown of some of my favourite well-known and more unusual nuts which you might consider stocking:

Almonds: Grown all over Europe. Excellent source of calcium, with a sweet flavour that is especially good in desserts and cakes but also goes well with fish and makes a lovely creamy

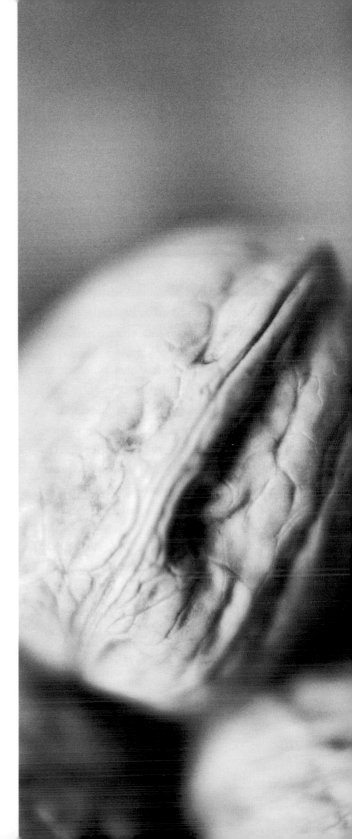

muesli, mixed nut and seed snacks, and can be added to breads.

For seeds used mainly as spices and flavourings in cooking (e.g. caraway or coriander seeds), see *Flavourers and cooking aids*, page 74; and for seed oils, see *Oils and fats*, page 68.

NUT AND SEED TIPS

The high unsaturated-oil content of nuts means that with long storage, particularly in heat and light, they are inclined to go rancid (taste 'off'). Nuts in their shells will store better and keep longer than shelled ones, but all nuts should be kept in cool, dry, dark conditions in an airtight tin. Shell nuts before eating.

Shelled nuts will store and keep better if they still have their brown skin on. Once the skins are removed, they are called blanched nuts.

Whole nuts will store and keep better than broken, chopped or ground ones.

Grind nuts yourself as you want them in a coffee-grinder. Ground nuts can be used as a part-substitute for flour in certain recipes (e.g. crumble toppings, sweet pastries).

Nut skins are usually quite edible (and will improve the fibre content of the nut) but sometimes recipes require them to be blanched. To remove skins, pour boiling water over the nuts briefly, then drain and rub off with your fingers.

If you do want toasted nuts for a recipe, toast your own. Just roast or dry-fry your blanched nuts until they take on a light golden colour, then remove them immediately from the heat source as they will quickly burn if left too long. Light toasting is preferable, as subjecting nuts to dry heat until they turn brown means that the essential unsaturated fats they contain may oxidize and will no longer be good for you.

You can harvest your own seeds from some of the plants in your garden.

Sunflowers ripen to seed in the autumn – if you don't want to leave them all for the birds, you can take them from the flat faces of the dead flowers, dry them in a sunny place or in a low oven, then remove the black-ish shells and there you have your own free sunflower seeds.

Similarly, get your own pumpkin or squash seeds by removing the seeds from fully ripened fruits (don't throw them away!) and treating them in the same way.

Cheese

There is very little choice if you want cheese to keep in the storecupboard, apart from chunks of feta in oil, various brands of which come in jars. You can also get jars of canapé-type products such as sweet chilli peppers stuffed with cream cheese.

If you have a very cool larder you may get away with keeping very hard mature cheeses, such as Parmesan, in the cupboard rather than the fridge. Ready-grated Parmesan in tubs, produced for the storecupboard, are in my opinion not worth the bother, but you may find them better than nothing.

Long-store fresh foods

If your food storage facilities consist of a few cupboards in a warm kitchen, then you may prefer to skip over this little section. However, if you are lucky enough to have a cool kitchen with enough space, or, even better, a proper larder, or, equally as good, another little-used dry but cool covered area such as a garage, shed, understairs area or unused, unheated spare bedroom – read on, because I'm about to give you some good news!

There are many – or at least several – fresh vegetables and spices, and indeed some fruits, which will keep for weeks, if not months, in such conditions, and so I like to describe them as larder vegetables. Here are some that you can grow (or buy in season from your local market or shop) and store for long periods without a fridge:

Onions: Maincrops onions, if well grown in good, warm, dry conditions, can last for several months if kept in a dry area. Many people string them up and hang them in a dry garage. Shallots also keep very well. When buying seed onions or onion seed, check that the variety you choose is described as a good storer.

Squash and pumpkin: Squashes and pumpkin harvested in the autumn, such as Crown Prince, butternut and many other types, will store very well. In general, the larger the pumpkin and the tougher the skin, the longer it will keep. As an example, I harvest in early October and next April

I still have usable pumpkins sitting on my back porch windowsill (if they haven't all been eaten, of course!). Summer squashes don't store very well, so eat them up within a couple of weeks.

Potatoes, beets, carrots, parsnips, swede: Root vegetables can be stored as described on page 60, in layers, in boxes, in a dark, dry, cool place, and should keep until late winter.

Apples, pears: As root vegetables, but may only last until around Christmas.

Quinces: Will keep for months.

Spices: Some spices, such as fresh garlic bulbs and ginger roots, will keep for weeks. Keep garlic bulbs whole, not split into cloves, in a container with holes in it (you can buy special garlic containers if you want, but even a little cardboard box with holes in it will be fine), and buy large pieces of ginger complete with all the skin. Whole chillies will keep if you lay them in a shallow dish in a dry place – over time they will dry out and can be used as dried chillies.

Other items: Some other foods which you might have thought needed refrigeration can in fact manage perfectly well for a couple of weeks, or even more, in a cool area in the kitchen or larder. Good examples are eggs (some people say that eggs should *not* be kept in the fridge) and mature deli sausages and hams. Eggs straight from the hen should keep in a coolish place for at least

three weeks, while cured sausages, if you hang them with plenty of dry air circulating around, can last longer than that. Check now and again to make sure all is OK.

Herbs and spices

No modern larder is complete without a good range of spices, most of which dry and keep very well. Herbs are less successful, but some work better than others. Spices store better and retain their aroma for much longer if you keep them as whole seeds, roots or sticks. A small coffee- or spice-grinder will grind down what you need in a few seconds, or you can pound them with pestle and mortar. Whole spices are easy to find on the net or in delis and health-food stores, while some supermarkets also stock a reasonable range.

If you must buy your spices ready-ground, then buy the smallest amounts available and store them in a dark, dry place. If you have to have a spice rack displaying your herbs and spices in the kitchen, then please do choose opaque containers, not see-through glass jars, as you must avoid the light getting on either herbs or spices.

Whole books have been written on both spices and herbs, so there is room here only to give you a rundown of those individual spices and herbs which I personally use a lot and wouldn't want to be without. You may have others to add to the list.

In addition, there are almost endless combinations of herbs and spices available – ready-blended dry mixes for dozens of different styles of dish, from jerk through Thai and Indian curries to stir-fry seasonings. In most homes, these will go stale way before they are used up, so stick with just two or three favourites. In my kitchen I have Chinese five spice, garam masala, herbes de Provence and mixed peppercorns. I list a few of my favourite brands in the A–Z under Herbs and also Spices (pages 238 and 246). Blends are mostly quite

easy to make yourself (see box, page 65), as and when you want them, from the basic herbs and spices (perhaps with the addition of other ingredients such as a little salt). Garam masala is particularly easy to make.

Most herbs and spices are rich sources of antioxidants – vitamin-like compounds found in plants which can offer protection against disease and the signs of ageing. Even used in small amounts, they make a significant contribution to antioxidant intake. They also individually contain different elements which can have health benefits. For example, chillies contain capsaicin, a pain reliever, while ginger contains gingerols which can ease nausea and help digestion.

Spices

Allspice: The berry of a tree from the Caribbean, it gets its name because it tastes of cinnamon, nutmeg and cloves. Combine some ground allspice with a little orange juice, soft brown sugar and groundnut oil and spread it on to gammon slices before grilling. Sprinkle into fruit compotes, such as plum, apple or pear.

Note: Don't confuse allspice (a berry) with mixed spice (a combination of several ground spices often used in fruit cakes).

Caraway: The caraway plant is a member of the parsley family. Its seeds have a slight aniseed flavour and they are great with all kinds of vegetables, including cabbage and carrots, and are a traditional ingredient of seed cake (a plain sponge flavoured with seeds before cooking) and the Moroccan harissa paste.

Cardamom: This herbacious perennial plant comes from southern India and Sri Lanka – the dried dark seeds inside pale green seed pods (which shouldn't be eaten) have a strong, almost citrus taste. It is used in garam masala, so is essential if you make your own. Cardamom seeds can be added to rice dishes such as kedgeree.

Chilli: Members of the capsicum family, there are hundreds of varieties of these seed pods in all shapes, sizes and degrees of heat. The milder ones can be popped into all kinds of savoury stews and sauces to give a bit more interest, while the hotter ones are the traditional addition to classics such as chilli con carne and other Mexican cuisine, and Indian and Thai curries. Most chillies start out on the plant green, and gradually turn to red as they ripen. This is why dried chilli is always red – you need to dry the fully ripe fruit (if you want to preserve green chilli, then de-seed it, chop it roughly and freeze it or preserve it in oil).

You can dry fresh chillies easily yourself – either shop-bought or home-grown ones – in a dry, hot room, spread out or on a baking tray in a very low oven. You can also buy dried whole chillies and grind them yourself, or use them whole (remove before serving) in spicy stews, curries and so on. If you are a huge fan of chilli, it's worth seeking out some of the more unusual dried varieties on the market (see A–Z).

Chilli is widely available ground, crushed in dried form, and also crushed and preserved in little jars with some oil. Cayenne pepper is, basically, chilli pepper by another name.

Note: Chilli powder may be a blend of spices and may come in mild or hot varieties. If you are unsure, read the ingredients label.

The heat of chillies is measured using Scoville units – with around 3,000 being mild, 10,000 getting warm and 300,000 so hot you can't eat it! Even touching a very hot raw chilli with your fingers and then licking them can cause mouth burn. Take care when using hot raw chillies and avoid rubbing your eyes, etc. – wash your hands thoroughly afterwards or, even better, use surgical gloves and discard them.

Cinnamon: With a warm, sweet aroma, this is the dried and curled bark of a tree that grows in the Far East. It is best to buy the whole sticks as they keep much better than ground cinnamon. Whole sticks can be popped into dishes (e.g. fruit compote, rice pudding) and removed before serving, or you can grind up sticks and use in garam masala, hot drinks (e.g. mulled wine or hot chocolate), lamb stews (e.g. tagines, Turkish stews) or in biscuits and fruit cakes.

Cloves: Unopened, dried flower buds of an Indonesian tree. Keep whole cloves, not the ground type. They are very strong, so use just a few when a recipe requires it. Typical uses are to flavour apples and pears for pies; in mulled wine

and punch; stuck into gammon before roasting; and in hearty meat and game casseroles. If you put them into dishes whole, always remove them before serving. Sometimes ground cloves are an ingredient of garam masala.

Coriander seed: Coriander is an easy-to-grow annual plant – eat the leaves and when the plant begins to go to seed (as it will do, quite quickly) leave the flowers to turn into your own coriander seed – harvest by placing a bag underneath the seed heads when they have turned brown. Coriander seed is one of the most useful spices you can keep – grind the little seeds when you need them as they quickly lose flavour when ground. The seeds go particularly well with mushrooms (e.g. in the starter or salad mushrooms à la Grecque), lentils and pork (add to

Herbs

Not many herbs are worth keeping in a dry state as they lose most of their aroma and flavour. Here are the few that I find do keep OK in an airtight tin. Use them in any recipe that requires fresh herbs, but reduce the quantity as the drying process concentrates the flavour somewhat.

Bay leaves: Just pick the leaves off a bay tree and lay them out in a cool oven or on paper in a warm dry place, and leave them until they are dried. Use one large leaf or two smaller leaves in family meat and fish casseroles; add to the milk with which you are going to make savoury white sauces; or add to oil marinades.

Oregano/marjoram: The little leaves are delicious with many Mediterranean lamb dishes such as moussaka, good under the skin of roast chicken, on pizza, in tomato sauce, in rice stuffings for aubergines, and in a herb omelette along with, perhaps, thyme, mint and sage.

Rosemary: Goes well with roast lamb (make slits in the meat and stuff with slivers of garlic and rosemary leaves), oily fish and chicken, and is a useful addition to meat and fish marinades.

Sage: Great for stuffings, pasta, and in mixed herbs for eggs, chicken and pork.

Thyme: Ingredient of the classic bouquet garni, and of mixed herbs and herbes de Provence. Great with chicken and game, and brings out the best in many casseroles and British stews. Add to breadcrumb and rice stuffings for chicken and pork.

HERB DRYING

If you grow your own herbs, it is easy to dry all of the above. Strip oregano and thyme from their stalks and dry them in a very low oven for half an hour.

Pick rosemary stalks whole, tie them with fine string and hang them on any hook in the kitchen to dry out naturally. You can pick and dry your own bouquet garni in little bunches, tied with string, to pop into your stews (fish them out using the string before serving) – much tastier than the kind in teabag-type sachets. These usually contain bay leaf, oregano and thyme, but you can vary them to suit your dishes. Usually just hanging up the bunches in the kitchen will dry them out well enough, unless your kitchen is particularly damp or cold.

HERBS THAT DON'T DRY WELL

Basil, chervil, chives, dillweed, coriander leaf, mint (but see page 199), parsley and tarragon. For most of these, you can instead preserve them in oil (see Chapter 9) and I have even frozen parsley and tarragon, both of which are fine as long as you just want the flavour and aroma in stews, soups, etc., rather than to use in fresh salads or as a garnish.

Oils and fats

Oils for the kitchen can come from a wide variety of plants. They may be extracted from seeds (such as sunflower seeds, rapeseeds, sesame seeds), nuts (peanuts (groundnuts), walnuts, hazelnuts, almonds, for instance), pulses (for example, soya beans), grains (such as rice bran oil) or fruit (for instance olives, avocados).

Because of their high unsaturated fat content, most oils are liquid at room temperature, unlike butter, lard and hard margarines, which are solid at room temperature because of their high saturated and/or hydrogenated fat content. Using more good-quality plant oils and less of these hard fats may be better for our health, as they may lower LDL blood cholesterol and may offer other forms of protection because of the vitamins and antioxidants they may contain.

Depending on how the oil is harvested and processed, it may contain low or high levels of beneficial compounds. The cheapest cooking oils, often simply labelled 'blended vegetable oil', go through a brutal solvent-extraction method where the very high heats, chemical solvents, bleaches and deodorizers used will not only remove the oils' natural colour, aroma and flavour but also their nutrients. They are unlikely to have any beneficial compounds remaining in them.

Oils are also an important nutrient for healthy skin, hair and joints. So, for both health and sensory reasons, when choosing oils it pays to know what the different terms on the labels mean (they can apply to any type of plant oil, not just olive oil).

Cold pressed: No form of heating or refining was used during extraction, which should mean a good-quality oil. However, due to the pressing process, heat is still formed – cold-pressing can mean temperatures of up to around 50°C (if a cold-pressing system called expeller-pressed is used), although some cold-pressed oils are made in the traditional way (literally, pressed) which creates less heat – typically up to 25°C. Some labels will tell you which method of cold-pressing was used. Cold-pressed oils are usually some of the most expensive and should be high in antioxidants.

First pressing: The oil that is extracted from the plant the first time it is pressed. This first pressing is another good indication of quality and antioxidant content, and the oil will usually be rich in colour and flavour. Further pressings – a second or even a third – are often achieved, but with each pressing the nutrients and strength of colour and flavour are likely to reduce.

Extra-virgin: A term used for olive oil, which is similar to the first pressing. Extra-virgin olive oil should have an acidity less than 0.8g per 100g of oil.

Single estate: Most of the oil that we buy is similar to much of the wine that we buy, in that it is usually blended from more than one growing estate, often from more than one area, and sometimes from more than one country. Thus 'single estate' is an exclusive and expensive oil, grown on one farm and bottled there too, which should have its own distinctive estate flavour, colour and aroma and, as with wine grapes, there may be good years and bad years. True oil buffs may know their years just as wine experts do.

Organic: Crops for kitchen oils are regularly sprayed with pesticides, which are fat-soluble and therefore likely to be present in the oil. You can buy organic oils (see A–Z) which will not have been sprayed with the wide range of chemicals allowed on non-organic crops. Organic oils should also be virtually GM-free.

Acidity: A low acidity level is an indicator of the quality of the oil.

If the oil you are looking at doesn't contain any of the above words, then it is likely to be a lower-quality oil with a mild flavour.

What oils do you need?

The number of different oils that you regularly stock in the larder will depend somewhat on the type of cooking that you do and what you like to eat. So the list below is here to help you, rather than as a 'must have' list. But basically your larder oils can be divided into those you use for high-heat cooking (e.g. shallow and deep frying, stir-frying, browning meat or sautéing onions for casseroles) and those you use cold (e.g. for salad dressings, drizzling, dips and sauces).

For cooking, there is no need to waste money on the top-end oils described above. First of all, they lose much of their special flavour and characteristics when heated; second, they have a much lower smoke point than more refined oils, in part because of the various remnants of the original plant that they contain – i.e. they are not highly refined. (But different refined oils also have different smoke points.)

For high-heat cooking, you want to use an oil with a high smoke point – not only because if you get to the stage where your cooking oil is getting a blue haze or actually smoking, the food will not taste good, but also because this means that the oil has broken down, lost its stability and is 'oxidizing'. That, simplified, means the opposite of its good, antioxidant effect, and it can actually have an adverse effect on your health. Regular use of oxidized oils has been linked with cancer, for example. Each time you re-use plant oils at a high temperature, their smoking point is lowered as they oxidize a bit more, so you should try to use fresh oil each time you fry – and don't fry your food until it is dark brown; a light gold is the maximum colour to aim for.

For low-heat cooking or cold recipes, I would,

however, urge you to consider buying the best oils you can afford as they do make a difference to your dishes, from a simple oil to drizzle over fish or bread, through salad dressings and sauces.

I would save the very top-end single-estate oils literally for use as a special treat where their characteristics are given a chance to shine: drizzle them over cooked fish, meat or steamed vegetables, use them to garnish soups or pasta, drizzle over a leaf salad rather than using a classic dressing. Then use slightly less dazzlingly expensive, but still good-quality, oils for vinaigrettes and other dressings and for pasta sauces and so on.

For making your own mayonnaise, I would not use 100 per cent olive oil as this produces a very strong-tasting result; I would go for a lighter oil such as sunflower, or use half of a mildish non-virgin olive oil (preferably one labelled 'light') to half sunflower or safflower oil.

Lastly, I would try to use oils produced and bottled in the UK, or from our near Mediterranean and European neighbours, to save on transport costs and boost our own oil-producing effort. Hempseed oil and rapeseed oil are two that can be easily produced in the UK. Soya bean oil and peanut (groundnut) oil are likely to have come from much further away.

Olive oil: Unlike most other plant oils, which are higher in polyunsaturated fats, olive oil is high in mono-unsaturated fats – now thought to be even better for heart health and blood cholesterol than the polyunsaturates. It is also high in vitamin E.

Early-harvest olive oil suggests a greener, more peppery flavour than late-harvest oil. Extra-virgin olive oils from the first pressings will have a low acidity level of below 1 per cent. Sometimes you will find not extra-virgin, but just virgin olive oil. This means the oil has an acidity below 1.5 per cent. Bottles just marked 'olive oil' are likely to have gone through a hot pressing and are likely to be blended (see above) and to have a higher acidity level. Bottles labelled 'light' olive oil are specially blended and refined to have a subtler flavour and are more suitable for use in cooked dishes and for mayonnaise.

PDO/PGI is an assurance that the oil has come from the country stated on the bottle. Olive-oil enthusiasts will go for oils from particular countries, or even areas of countries, or particular estates, and the oils do vary tremendously in characteristics from country to country. It's a good idea to use an oil from the country of your recipe, if that is appropriate (for instance, a Spanish olive oil with a paella, an Italian oil with a pasta dish).

In addition, olive oils can be described with certain words, similar to wine:

- *fruity oils* have a strong olive flavour
- *pizzico* means the oil has medium to strong peppery notes
- *grassy oils* have a fresh, more savoury, 'light green' flavour
- *hay flavour oils* have a dry, herby bouquet and flavour

English mustard – a mix of brown and white seeds with added turmeric – as a table condiment is not for the faint-hearted, being extremely pungent, but a little added to a béchamel sauce will lift it, and the classic use is to make dry mustard powder up with water and smear it all over the fat of a gammon before roasting.

French mustards, such as the creamy, medium-hot Dijon; Meaux, which is made from mixed mustard seeds; and thick brown Bordeaux (sometimes, confusingly, just called French mustard) are all worth a place in the larder. My favourite is Dijon, in both its smooth and wholegrain guises, as it is a perfect pep-up for ham, sausages, grilled calves' or lambs' liver and deli meats such as pastrami. It is even more useful in adding depth to savoury sauces, coating meats before cooking, in marinades and in salad dressings, including mayonnaise.

I don't bother with *American mustard*, but you might if you like hotdogs.

Bottled sauces have a poor reputation and yet I find all the following very useful, both for putting on the table and for adding here and there to recipes: sweet chilli, tomato ketchup, plum sauce, hoisin sauce, Worcestershire sauce and soya sauce (these last two contain a great deal of salt and should be used very sparingly). The best soya sauce is one called tamari – it is made without wheat, whereas most of the others include wheat. I find it has a superior flavour. Soya can be used if you've run out of Worcestershire sauce.

Sweet sauces can be useful, but care needs to be taken over quality. A bottle of fruit coulis and a bottle of chocolate sauce are both a good idea – but see the A–Z for buying ideas.

Lastly, I keep a few jars of *relishes, chutneys* and *pickles*. Cumberland sauce is a happy marriage of redcurrant jelly with port wine and orange juice which is brilliant with lamb, gammon, pheasant and goose; horseradish sauce (a mix of grated horseradish root and cream, sometimes with other flavours) is mandatory with roast beef and is absolutely brilliant with smoked mackerel, and unless you grow your own horseradish it isn't always possible to make it yourself. To that I would add some Indian pickles and chutneys, especially Brinjal (aubergine) pickle, mild and hot mango chutneys, and some British fruit-based chutneys – apple (preferably locally made) being my favourite; it's better than anything else with Cheddar cheese.

Cooking sauces, marinades and pastes

Everything I have said about having some ready-made table condiments in your larder also applies to this category. Yes, I am sure we can all make our own tomato sauce and whizz up a pesto, but sometimes it really does help when you're busy or tired to have a good-quality ready-made version in the cupboard.

Some of the items I feel no guilt in stocking include:

- Ready-made tomato-based sauces in jars – plain basic tomato sauce can be jazzed up with some fresh herbs or chilli.

- Sundried tomato purée, tomato purée, red pesto, basil pesto.

- Fish sauce (nam pla), mushroom ketchup, oyster sauce.

- Harissa paste, ketjap manis (delicious Indonesian condiment similar to dark soya sauce but sweeter and richer, which is ideal in marinades or in Indonesian recipes, or as a substitute for soya sauce).

- Jars of ready-made curry blends or pastes are handy: Thai red and green curry paste, and one hot (e.g. rogan josh) and one mild (such as balti) Indian curry paste are the basics. You can adapt or improve these by adding a few other ingredients of your choice. For instance, when I have to resort to a Thai green curry paste, I add a stick of lemon grass and one or two of my own chopped green chillies and some garlic.

- Marinade ingredients: storecupboard items that can be used in marinades include honey, oil, vinegar, mustard, dried chilli flakes, soya sauce, ketchup and Worcestershire sauce, as well as spice pastes.

Pastry products: You can buy ready-made pastry cases and crumble mixes which vary very much in quality from brand to brand.

Dried potato powder: Seems to have fallen out of favour even with busy mums of small children, but you can still buy packs of this white powder which, when made up, turns into a rather glutinous mass of starch. If you make it up carefully, though, and don't use too much water, it can be OK for potato cakes, fishcakes and to thicken stews.

Packet stuffings: Usually a disappointing mix of dry crumbs, dried herbs and little else except salt – but some speciality varieties can make a standby, especially if you jazz them up with extra herbs or seasoning.

Lazy garlic, ginger and chilli: These little jars of spices and garlic are widely used now instead of the real, fresh thing. They are OK, I suppose, but – as with much produce in jars – once opened they need to be stored in the fridge.

Ready lemon and lime juice: Little plastic containers with juice mixed with preservatives. I would need to be quite desperate to use these, as I don't find their flavour very good, but I suppose if lemon or lime juice is 100 per cent vital to your recipe and you have nothing fresh, they could do a job of sorts.

Mayonnaise: To people who have been brought up on jars of ready mayonnaise, the taste of real, home-made mayo can be quite a shock. Conversely, to those who always make their own, these jars of white, bland spooning sauce are not mayonnaise at all. However, if you have a jar of good-quality mayonnaise in your cupboard you can in an emergency jazz it up, perhaps with some lemon juice (if you have any!) and beat in a little good olive oil to make it taste more authentic. You can also liven up bought mayo with chopped capers and garlic to serve with trout or salmon, or as a dip with breadsticks and crudités, or beat in some tapenade or basil pesto for a dip.

Fish and meat pâtés: Some of the little pâtés and pastes in jars and pots are not too bad at all – especially the strong-tasting types such as crab and tuna. If you are short of a starter, you can mix them with fromage frais, thick yogurt or cream cheese for a dip.

3 LARDER PRACTICALITIES

Many of us have forgotten how to look after a larder. While choosing or making the right foods for it and for you is of course important, you also need to look after everything properly to maximize its shelf-life and get the most out of your stocks. Most of us also need to maximize our available space. This chapter is concerned with all these practicalities.

In today's homes, a larder can be anything from a couple of cupboards above the kitchen base units, through a floor-to-ceiling cupboard in the same room, to a large, old, purpose-built larder somewhere near the kitchen of an old house. Whatever space you have for your larder, you need to use it well and look after the area properly. Hopefully, the larger your family the larger your availabe food-storage area will be.

Clearing and cleaning your larder

In truth, most of us waste around a third of our available cupboard space by keeping out-of-date tins and packets, and items we are just never going to use. So the first thing to do is set aside a couple of hours one wet weekend to take out absolutely everything you have, put it all on the kitchen table and rationalize it, then give the larder a thorough clean before replacing only the things you really want to keep and should keep.

Before you do this, you should gather all the cleaning equipment you need – which may be nothing more than some non-contaminating wet wipes for a small cupboard up to vacuum cleaner, mop, dusters and so on for larger areas. And you should also make sure you have plenty of containers – airtight lidded tins or plastic containers, for example, in a variety of sizes.

Take everything out individually, read the use-by dates and discard everything that goes beyond a month or two past its use-by date. Discard everything in packets or tins that are broken or damaged, and any dry goods, such as flour, that have been around longer than a couple of months. For things that don't fit into either of these categories but that you know you will never use, put them into a bag and give them away another day.

Now you need to clean the larder thoroughly with a suitable cleaner (a mild solution of sugar

soap would do well) and plenty of hot water. Let the shelves dry thoroughly with open doors before attempting to replace anything – if you put items such as bags or card packets of flour or sugar on damp shelves, they will ruin.

Pests

You also need to inspect the larder for any signs of life! Especially in darker, larger cupboards, have a good close inspection for nasties such as silverfish, mouse droppings, insects and so on.

Prevention is the main key here. Try to match your buying to your usage so that you don't have lots of packets of dry loose goods, such as bags of flour and cereal grains, hanging round for long periods.

Also, be careful where you buy. Go for shops with a high turnover rate and whose premises look clean and well kept. I have before now got items home and found them already infested with bugs.

Check your food frequently and carefully for signs of infestation. Pests can infest some surprising things – the larder beetle, for instance, can live on pepper. Keeping a clean larder with all foods well covered and with good hygiene should mean you can eliminate most or all pests most or all of the time – or at least, if they do find their way to your home, they will not find anything to eat and won't stay around long. That's the idea!

Also, don't put live pests in your kitchen bin as they can escape!

In the box opposite I list the main culprits you may find in larders or kitchens throughout the country.

Ants: These can get into your kitchen via open doors and windows, looking for food, especially sweet food (they follow the scent). Make sure they can't find anything. Kill them on windowsills, doorsteps, etc., with boiling water.

Biscuit beetle larvae: The larvae of the tiny, red biscuit beetle eat flour, grains, bread, biscuits and seeds. Can be controlled with insecticidal powder (see *Silverfish*).

Cockroaches: Large, black, scuttling creatures that hide away in dark cracks and corners. Cockroaches will feed on almost any foodstuff and can carry dysentery, typhoid and gastro-enteritis. (See also *Rats*.)

Flies: Come in via open windows and doors. Most make a lot of noise so you can quickly grasp the problem, but blowflies or bluebottles are very quiet and may creep into the larder without your realizing. Keep doors shut all the time throughout summer – flies tend to disappear in winter, though our recent milder winters mean they have a longer season. They will lay eggs on fresh food, especially meat, so be careful to cover everything up and clear away food scraps as soon as possible. Keep wastebins as far away from the larder and working area of the kitchen as you can and empty them frequently. Keep work surfaces, tables, etc., spotlessly clean. Flies and other insects love to lay eggs in tiny scraps of food that they can find but which may not be easily seen by you.

I dislike using fly sprays as I hate the smell and most are aerosols, which are not environmentally friendly. Fly-catching strips are available, but they don't look very attractive! You can buy electrical flycatchers, but they use electricity and again are not a pretty sight. If you are in a high fly area (say, near a cattle farm) you could cover your windows and doors in the summer with fixed nets, as they do in parts of the USA and Australia.

Flour beetles: These 3–4mm reddish-brown beetles (and their larvae) feed on flour and milled grains, but they'll also eat a wide range of other dry products in the cupboard. They don't spread disease but can be a real nuisance once you are infested and all you can really do is throw the infested foods away (outside the home).

Flour mites: An 0.5mm (that's tiny) pale brown mite that can infest bags of flour. They like a moist, warm atmosphere, so try to keep your larder as dry and cool as possible. Don't use flour infested with mites.

Flour moth larvae: Eats flour but also a range of other foods such as nuts and dried fruit. Small, white, wriggling larvae, sometimes inside a silk 'nest'.

Grain weevils: Not often found in domestic larders but will eat sunflower seeds, flour, cereals and grains (but not pasta). Brownish colour and about 0.5cm long with a long 'snout'. They don't fly.

Larder beetles: Blackish-brown beetle about 1–1.5cm long, with a yellowish patch on the back containing six black spots. Eats high-protein foods, including stored cooked meats. Can be killed with insecticidal powder (see *Silverfish*).

Mice: Small black droppings are usually the first sign – or sometimes you will hear scratching-type noises when the home is quiet. (See also *Rats* below.)

Rats: Can get into surprisingly small spaces. If you live in an old home, it pays to make sure the cupboards, kitchen and skirting, etc., are well maintained.

For cockroaches, mice and rats it may pay to get in a specialist pest-controller to rid you of the problem.

Silverfish: Tiny fish-like creatures in silver to grey, which thrive in damp, dark conditions and places that are little disturbed. You can sprinkle silverfish-control powder around your cupboards (after emptying them) to kill them before cleaning thoroughly and then re-stocking.

Health in your storecupboard

Most of us today are concerned not only with saving money and reducing waste but, of course, with eating healthily. I perceive that many people feel that things kept in the fridge often provide a healthier diet than menus planned around the larder.

I guess that thinking comes because we view a fridge as full of vitamin C-rich salads, fruit and fresh vegetables, healthy yogurts and fresh lean meats and fish. Of course that view is correct, but it isn't the whole picture. I am not implying that you should give up on fresh fruit and vegetables – not at all: they are, indeed, our best source of vitamin C and provide antioxidants, colour, flavour and variety to the plate. But of course there are plenty of unhealthy things that can be found in a fridge too – think chilled desserts, cream cakes, high-salt, high-fat chilled ready meals, cream cheese and so on.

A well-stocked larder, on the other hand, can contain all you need for a healthy diet just as easily as a fridge. Here is a list of the nutrients we need in our diets and which larder items can provide them:

Energy (calories): This is provided by all foods and drinks except water.

Carbohydrates: Rice and all grains, pasta, breakfast cereals, sugar, honey, pulses.

Protein: Pulses, nuts, seeds, canned fish.

Fats: Healthy fats are found in some pulses, nuts, seeds (and their oils), oily canned fish, olive oil.

Vitamins: Vitamin C is found in small amounts in canned vegetables and fruits (the canning process destroys some of the original vitamin C), in longlife vegetable soups and casseroles, in canned tomatoes, passata, tomato sauces and in some longlife juices such as orange juice. There should also be some in fruit preserves, especially if home made and light-set. You can also sprout pulses and seeds for vitamin C.

Vitamin B group are found in wholegrains, pulses, breakfast cereals, canned fish, canned or jar pâtés, Marmite (yeast extract), nuts and seeds, dried mushrooms.

Vitamin E is found in good quantity in plant oils, nuts, seeds and tomato purée.

Vitamin D is contained in canned fish and in fortified breakfast cereals.

Vitamin A (from beta-carotene) is found in tomato products, and canned red peppers, carrots, spinach, mango.

Minerals: Calcium is found in nuts and seeds, dried fruits, canned sardines, muesli.

Iron is found in dried fruits, spices, fortified breakfast cereals, wholegrains, pulses.

Zinc, magnesium and selenium are found in nuts and seeds, canned seafood and other larder goods.

Dietary fibre: Found in whole grains, dried fruit, pulses, canned fruits and vegetables.

So as you can see, you could live healthily from your larder for a long time if need be. The best idea is to supplement your larder with judicious buying of regular amounts of fresh produce. If you can't shop for much fresh stuff, then go for items that will provide you with maximum important nutrients for minimum weight and expense. These might be:

- Berries, sweet peppers, dark green leafy salad and cabbage-type vegetables, and citrus fruit for vitamin C, fibre, carotenes and antioxidants.

- Small oily fish portions such as salmon or mackerel fillets for omega-3 oils.

- Natural bio yogurt for calcium and pro-biotics.

- Small amounts of lean red meat and organic chicken for iron and a wide range of vitamins and minerals.

- And if you don't stock your own bread flour and make bread, then add a wholegrain loaf for energy, fibre and a range of vitamins and minerals.

You need of course to keep an eye out for some potential problems when stocking the larder.

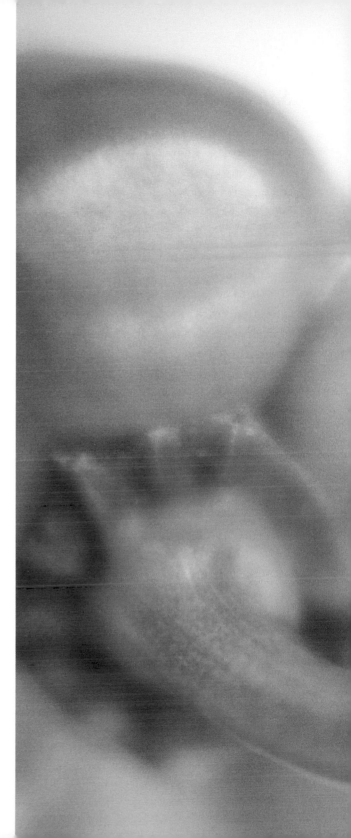

Food safety

There is probably less opportunity for giving yourself food poisoning by cooking from a well-run larder than there is from living out of the fridge, which, because of the apparent cool temperature, gives people a sense of security which is often unjustified. Most fridges are not kept at a cool enough temperature and cross-contamination, fungi on forgotten leftovers and so on can make the average fridge a real hotbed of potential poisons! An ideal temperature for a domestic fridge is 3–4°C, with 5°C as a maximum.

However, you still need to be aware of some simple guidelines if you are to be a larder cook with peace of mind.

- Keep the larder clean and pest-free (see pages 85–7).

- Keep all the food you can in its own suitable container. This will usually mean an airtight tin or box or jar. This is to avoid spoilage, drying out, contamination by bugs, insects, etc.

- Once most cans and jars have been opened, if there are leftovers they need to be transferred to a lidded container and kept in the fridge. The exception to this is most commercial preserves (jams, marmalades), pickles, chutneys and table sauces. Some cooking sauces in bottles (e.g. plum sauce, hoisin sauce) are fine in the cupboard. Once cans are opened, if the contents are just kept in the can (even in the fridge) chemicals from the inside of the can lining may leach into the food.

- Keep opened bottles and jars clean. Wipe and dry pouring lids before putting them back in the cupboard after use.

- Check with your eyes that a food is in good condition and pest-free before using it. Flour mites (see page 87), for instance, can even get into some containers that you would think are completely airtight, and are quite hard to spot buried deep inside the flour – keep a sharp eye.

- Check dates on labels frequently. 'Use by' is the date to take notice of – this means that food should be eaten by that date at the latest. However, this notice is more often used on perishable goods such as those kept in the fridge.

- 'Best before' is more often found on larder goods with a longer shelf-life. This notice means that the food inside may be fine to eat after that date, which is only a guide. To be honest, I have opened and used cans of all kinds of things months and sometimes years after the best-before date and the contents have been fine. However, if you are using a product well past its best-before date you do need to be extra careful when examining the contents before eating.

- A simple test for best-before goods opened after their date is to look – does it look OK? – smell – does it smell good? – and then take a tiny taste. Does it taste OK? If you can answer yes to all of those, then the item is probably fine.

- Also remember that once a product is opened (e.g. a jar of jam) the best-before guide can no longer really apply, as an opened product will always last a shorter time than an unopened one.

- Items particularly likely to lose their individual, good characteristics if kept too long (even if they are still perfectly edible) include flour, grains and any dry goods.

- **If you have any doubts at all, throw it away.**

- If keeping eggs in a cool larder, rather than the fridge, eat them up as soon as you can – and go for eggs which have the Lion symbol on them as the hens that laid them will have been inoculated against salmonella, a common form of food poisoning associated with both chickens and eggs.

- If you use canned meat (e.g. corned beef, ham), be doubly careful before opening to check the can for any signs of damage and, once opened, look very carefully at the contents for any signs of discoloration, white patches (which aren't the natural fat of the meat) and so on. If you see anything that doesn't look good, throw the contents away. Very, very occasionally the meat-canning process can go awry, so you need to be on the lookout for that tiny chance you could have a rogue can.

- When cooking or preparing food with items from the larder which will be returned to the larder, make sure that you keep your hands clean and return containers to the larder wiped over with a mild disinfectant suitable for the kitchen. It is quite easy to cross-contaminate containers (which can migrate to the contents) when cooking. For example, if you are doing a chicken stir-fry, you might chop up your raw chicken. If you then get out a jar of chilli sauce from the cupboard and put it on to the chicken chopping board, you have potential cross-contamination with salmonella or other bugs. However busy cooking you are, you do have to think about kitchen hygiene.

Larder accessories

It is useful if you keep a stock of accessories that will be used frequently for your larder. These will include:

- A selection of hard containers with lids for items such as flour, grains, pasta. Plastic are the most useful, while tins can be fine as long as they don't get moist and then rusty.

- Glass jars with screw-top lids or kilner-type lids for all kinds of things, such as sugar, as well as preserves and bottling. Two or three different sizes are ideal.

- Opaque, small to medium jars for herbs and spices.

- Preserving equipment, including a preserving pan, long-handled spoons, tongs, muslin, sieves, funnel and preserving thermometer (not essential, though).

- Labels, felt-tipped pen, rubber bands, decorative tops for jars (if you make gifts for people), cellophane.

You will also of course keep some typical larder items on display in your kitchen, so you will have caddies for tea, coffee, sugar and perhaps a salt box.

SOME FINAL TIPS
Remember: don't overstock, especially for short-shelf-life items.
Think twice before you buy something on a whim.
Have concrete ideas for usage in your head before purchasing.
Check the larder through at least once a season to clean it out and re-assess its contents as above.

PART 2 Recipes

4 QUICK SNACKS AND STARTERS

Raiding the larder at the end of a busy day for something tasty to eat, or during the day for something that will fill a hungry moment or provide a no-cook snack, is something we all do.

Think of these moments as opportunities to eat something appetizing and healthy – not a quick snack about which you will feel guilty afterwards. One of the tricks is to have in your larder only items that are good, or at least relatively good, for you. Wholegrain crispbreads and rice cakes, healthier-than-crisps savoury snacks, protein-packed spreads (nut butters, for example) and toppings (I'm thinking home-made, reduced-sugar conserves) can fill a need for something instant, while it takes hardly any longer to make a blender hummus or bean purée.

In this chapter I've got together some of my favourite quick ideas, which can also be used for starters, as nibbles with drinks, or as part of a buffet.

All-larder snacks and suppers in less than 5 minutes

I don't pretend that these ideas are 'proper' recipes – but if you want something savoury to eat straight away and have followed my tips for stocking the larder in Chapter 1, then you should be able to rustle up at least one or two of these without any bother, even if the fridge is bare.

Couscous with Nuts, Seeds and Dried Fruit

Ⓥ

Reconstitute 50g (more if you are very hungry) of couscous in boiling vegetable or chicken stock (using a cube or Marigold bouillon), adding a small to medium handful of chopped dried apricots and 1 level tbsp of sultanas to the mix so that they soften up while the couscous absorbs the water.

When the couscous is ready, stir in 1 tbsp of flaked almonds, and 1 dsp each toasted pine nuts and shelled pistachios. You can eat this as it is, or drizzle in some oil-based dressing (see Chapter 7 for dressing ideas).

If you happen to have any fresh herb leaves on your windowsill, such as coriander or mint, adding a few to the couscous will liven up the flavour. And you can, of course, vary the nuts, seeds and dried fruit according to what you have.

Tuna and White Bean Pitta

Ⓥ

Take 1 wholemeal pitta bread, sprinkle it with water from the tap and put it in the toaster for a minute until hot and puffed up (or you can use the microwave on low for 30 seconds or so). Meanwhile, in a bowl combine the contents of a 100g can of tuna (well drained), 50g canned, drained cannellini beans, 1 tbsp chopped sundried tomatoes with their oil, and a pinch or two of smoked paprika. (You can use butterbeans instead of the cannellini, or a pinch of any other spice that takes your fancy.)

Split and fill the pitta with the mixture and eat. If you happen to have available any fresh tomatoes, red or spring onion or fresh parsley, then adding any of those to your pitta will increase your pleasure.

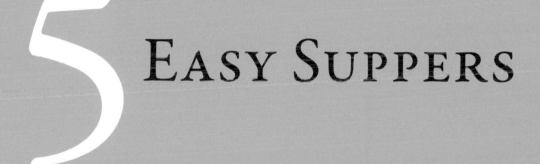

5 Easy Suppers

While it is wonderful to prepare a meal that cooks all day, or that involves many ingredients, and then sit down to a leisurely feast with family or friends, very often we all need a snack or meal that can be prepared quickly and with minimal fuss. This chapter contains my favourite recipes that will all perfectly fit the bill.

There are so many options if your cupboards are well-stocked. So try not to open the larder door then close it again and get a ready meal out of the freezer! As long as you have a selection of grains, tins of pulses and plenty of tomatoey things in cans and jars, some herbs and seasonings, you can always make a supper in 20 minutes or so which will be both delicious and good for you.

Should you also have some long-store fresh vegetables in the rack and a bit of cheese, then you do, indeed, have the wherewithal to make yourself a quick feast after all!

Falafel Patties with Piquillo Peppers

Serves 4 **V**

Fresh ingredients: onion, parsley, egg

1 large onion, peeled and finely chopped
2 tbsps light olive oil
2 cloves garlic, peeled and well crushed
350g jar or can piquillo peppers, drained and chopped (see Tip)
several dashes of Tabasco
2 x 400g cans chickpeas
1 tbsp finely chopped parsley
1 tsp each ground cumin and coriander seeds
1 egg, beaten
a little wholemeal flour
salt and black pepper

Add the onion and half the oil to a frying pan and sauté over medium-high heat for 8–10 minutes or until soft and transparent, stirring frequently, and adding the garlic for the last minute. Reserve half the onion mix in a bowl along with a quarter of the chopped piquillo peppers, then add the rest of the peppers to an electric blender along with the remaining onion mix from the frying pan, a dash of Tabasco and some seasoning to taste. Blend until smooth. Transfer back to the pan to reheat (or to a serving jug to heat in the microwave).

Drain the chickpeas and add them to a large mixing bowl with the parsley, spices, Tabasco to taste and some seasoning. Mash thoroughly with a fork (or you could mash in the blender, but a fork is just as easy as you don't need the mix too smooth). Now stir in the reserved onion and pepper mix, combining well, then add the egg. Form the mix into eight or twelve patties and dust with a little flour.

Fry the patties in the remaining oil for about 6–7 minutes, turning halfway through, until they are golden brown. Serve with the pepper sauce.

TIPS

Serve with some brown rice, couscous or bulghar wheat and a large green salad.

Note: piquillo peppers come in containers of varying sizes – don't worry too much if your can or jar contains a little less or more than the amount stated above. You can also use ordinary canned or bottled red peppers, if you like, though the piquillos do give a lovely flavour.

No-fuss Rice Pilaf

Serves 4 **V**

Fresh ingredients: coriander leaves, onion

600ml vegetable stock
1 sachet or tsp saffron threads
300g brown basmati rice
2 tbsps light olive oil
1 large onion, peeled and finely chopped
1 tsp each coriander and cumin seeds, lightly crushed
400g can chickpeas, drained and rinsed
75g each unsalted toasted cashews and flaked almonds
100g sultanas or raisins
bunch fresh coriander leaves

Heat the stock and saffron in a saucepan, stir well and add the rice. Bring to a gentle simmer, put the lid on and cook for 20 minutes or until the rice is tender.

Meanwhile, heat the oil in a large, non-stick frying pan and stir-fry the onion for 8 minutes over medium-high heat or until soft, transparent and just tinged with gold. Add the coriander and cumin seeds and stir to release the flavours, then add the chickpeas, nuts and sultanas and stir again for 2–3 minutes.

When the rice is ready (it shouldn't need draining), tip it into a serving bowl and stir in the onion mix. Garnish with coriander leaves before serving.

TIPS

You can add some chopped red pepper or courgette if you have any (add with the onion, or use canned or jarred ready-cooked – see A–Z).

While this pilaf makes a great vegetarian meal in itself, you can also use it in half quantities as a side dish for chicken or lamb tagine or a Turkish stew (see Chapter 6), or as part of a hot or cold buffet.

Storecupboard Tomato Sauce

Serves 4 ⓥ

Fresh ingredient: onion (optional)

2 tbsps light olive oil
1 large onion, peeled and finely chopped, or 1 can ready-fried onions
2 large juicy cloves garlic, peeled and well crushed, or 2 good tsps ready-minced garlic
400g can Italian chopped tomatoes
1 level tbsp sundried tomato paste
1 tsp soft brown sugar
salt and black pepper

Heat the oil in a large saucepan and sauté the onions (if using fresh) over a medium-high heat for 8 minutes or until soft and transparent, then add the garlic and stir for another minute. Add the rest of the ingredients, stir well, bring to a simmer, turn the heat down to low, and cook for 20 minutes or until you have a nice rich sauce. Check seasoning before using.

TIPS

The basic sauce is ideal as a pasta topping, perhaps with Parmesan.

The sauce is also a good base for further additions. You can add, for example, fresh chopped herbs, chilli (fresh or minced), sliced black or green olives, soya sauce, Worcestershire sauce or anchovies. You can also add firm white fish or shellfish.

The sauce will freeze or you could store it in an airtight jar (see Chapter 8).

Home-made Baked Beans

Serves 4

500g ready-cooked haricot beans (see Tip)
1 quantity Storecupboard Tomato Sauce (see previous recipe)
1 heaped tsp English mustard powder
1 tsp Dijon mustard
3 tsps soft dark brown sugar, or black treacle
2 tsps Worcestershire sauce
1 tbsp white wine vinegar
2 tsps balsamic vinegar

Put all ingredients in a heavy-based, lidded saucepan, stir well, bring to simmer, turn the heat down to low and cook, covered, for 30 minutes, stirring once or twice and adding a little boiling water if the sauce looks too thick towards the end of cooking time.

TIPS

Nice served with baked potatoes, any whole grain, or just on toast.

You can cook the beans in the oven, in a heavy-based casserole, if you like – in which case cook at around 170°C for 40 minutes, stirring halfway through and adding a little water if the sauce looks a bit thick.

You can buy cans of haricot beans, but you can also use canned, drained cannellini beans or a bean mix of your choice instead.

If you don't have any Storecupboard Tomato Sauce, you could use a large jar of good-quality ready-made tomato sauce for pasta, or even just a can of chopped tomatoes – the sauce will not be quite as tasty or rich but it will still be nice enough!

Rice and Beans

Serves 4 Ⓥ

Fresh ingredients: spring onions, red chilli, coriander leaves

600ml chicken stock
300g (dry weight) long-grain rice
large knob creamed coconut
1 jar roasted red peppers, drained and chopped
1 tbsp groundnut oil
2 cloves garlic, peeled and well crushed
6 spring onions, trimmed and chopped
1 large medium-hot red chilli, de-seeded and finely
    chopped
400g canned, drained black beans or other robust cooked
    beans (see Tip)
1 tbsp vinegar
1 tsp Tabasco
salt and black pepper to taste
bunch coriander leaves, de-stalked

Heat the stock in a saucepan and add the rice and coconut; bring to simmer and cook for 20 minutes or until the liquid is absorbed. Stir in the chopped peppers. Meanwhile, heat the oil in a frying pan and stir-fry the garlic, spring onions and chilli for a minute over medium heat. Add the beans, vinegar, Tabasco, a little salt and plenty of black pepper, and stir for a minute.

When the rice is cooked, mix the rice and beans in a serving bowl and gently stir in the coriander.

TIPS

You can use a little coconut cream from a can if you like, and extra cream can then be drizzled over the rice and beans to serve.

You can vary the beans – pinto, red kidney, mixed pulses or simple black beans can all be used. If you have dried beans, use the same weight of boiled, drained cooked beans. For instructions on cooking dried pulses, see the A–Z.

You can make this dish even quicker and simpler by using two 250g packets of 2-minute long-grain or basmati rice, heated according to packet instructions. Instead of the stock, stir 100ml coconut milk and half a crumbled chicken or vegetable stock cube into the frying pan after stir-frying the spices and stir for a minute before adding the beans and seasonings, then stir in the rice thoroughly, adding a little more coconut milk or hot water if the mix seems a little dry.

Quick Split-pea Soup

Serves 4

Fresh ingredients: onion, carrots, celery, ham

400g split peas
1 large onion, peeled and chopped
4 medium carrots, peeled and cut into 2cm chunks
2 sticks celery, roughly chopped
1 large bay leaf
1 litre ham stock (see Tip)
100g traditional ham, cut into strips
black pepper

Put the split peas, chopped vegetables, bay leaf and stock into a large pot and bring slowly to the boil. Simmer gently for about 25 minutes, or until the carrot is cooked but still firm.

Allow the soup to cool a bit, then remove the bay leaf and pour into an electric blender (this may need two batches) and whizz for half a minute or until you have a smooth soup, still with a few bits of vegetable in it for texture. Reheat, scatter the pieces of ham over the soup to serve and garnish with black pepper.

TIP

If you have more time, the traditional way to cook split-pea soup is to put the split peas and vegetables into water or light, low-salt vegetable stock with a smoked gammon piece (about 1kg in weight) and simmer for about 2 hours, then remove the meat joint and take the lean flesh off in strips. Blend the soup, then add the gammon bits back and reheat to serve.

Roast Marinated Cod with Butterbeans

Serves 4

Fresh ingredients: cod

700g cod fillet, or other white fish of choice (see Tip), cut into four
2 tsps ground saffron
1 tbsp ground sweet paprika
2–3 tsps ready-minced garlic, or 2 juicy cloves garlic, peeled and crushed
sea salt and black pepper
4 tbsps light olive oil
400g can butterbeans, drained and rinsed

Lay the fish in a non-metallic shallow dish in one layer. In a bowl, thoroughly combine the spices, garlic, salt and pepper with 2 tbsps of the olive oil and spoon over the cod. Rub the marinade in well, cover and leave for 20 minutes, or for up to 1 hour if you have time.

In a bowl, mash the butterbeans with the remaining olive oil and some salt and pepper, spoon into a lidded ovenproof dish and cover.

Remove the cover from the cod and roast in a preheated oven at 180°C for 15 minutes (or a little more, depending on the thickness of the fillets), basting once or twice. Put the butterbean dish, still with its lid on, on to a lower shelf of the oven to heat through (or you could use a microwave on high for 2 minutes).

When the cod is cooked through, serve with a spoonful of butterbean mash per piece.

TIPS

Avoid buying wild Atlantic cod, which is an endangered species of fish. You can find 'greener' cod or other white fish in most supermarkets and fishmongers. If your fishmonger is unable to tell you where your cod came from, you should shop elsewhere.

Buy Marine Stewardship Council (MSC)-certified, sustainably caught, or farmed organic cod; or if you can't get that, then you could use MSC-certified pollack, hoki, hake, coley or other white fish.

Nice served with some steamed broccoli, and/or some baked tomatoes if you have any (put them in the oven at the same time as the fish, on a small baking tray brushed with oil).

Don't marinate cod or other fish for longer than an hour, as the acids from the ingredients in the marinade will start to 'cook' the fish – even if there is no obvious acid in it such as lemon juice or vinegar. (If there is, the marinating time should be no more than half an hour.)

Pissaladière

Serves 4

Fresh ingredients: onions, bread

approx. 4 tbsps olive oil
1kg onions, peeled and thinly sliced
2 juicy cloves garlic, peeled and well crushed
salt and black pepper
4 slices wholemeal bread (see Tip)
12 anchovy fillets, drained and rinsed
12 stoned black olives, halved

Heat 3 tbsps of the oil in a very large pan and add
the onions. Stir well and cook slowly over a low
heat, stirring from time to time, until the onions
are very soft but not browned. This will take
half an hour. Add the garlic and some seasoning
towards the end of cooking.

When the onions are nearly ready, put the
remaining oil in another frying pan and fry the
bread slices on one side only, then place them on
the base of the grill pan, fried side down.

Spoon the onions over the top of the bread and
then arrange the anchovies and olives on top of
that. Drizzle over some more oil, add a little extra
seasoning, and grill under a medium heat for 5
minutes before serving.

TIPS

The key to pissaladière is to have the onions really soft
and almost caramelized, which can't be done over a hot
hob and takes more time than simply frying.

Instead of bread, you can use the same topping and
spread it over shortcrust or puff pastry, then bake in
the oven at 190°C for 20 minutes or until the pastry
is cooked.

6 MORE LEISURELY MEALS

Here are some nice meals for weekends or holidays, or for those evenings and lunchtimes when you don't need to rush. Some are nearly as easy as the Easy Suppers in Chapter 5, but maybe with a few more ingredients or slightly longer cooking time. Others will take several hours to cook but will be short on preparation or effort, and then there are a few that will be eminently suitable for a special occasion, or for when you just feel like cooking or trying something new.

I've included a variety of dishes for each season, such as traditional Turkish pilaf with dried fruits and nuts, mushroom risotto, ribolitto, pulse and grain casseroles, spiced hob dishes, oven roasts, pies and gratins and slow-cook soups and stews. As with many of my recipes, I try to cut down somewhat on the amount of meat and animal products that I use. In the West, we mostly eat far more protein than we really need.

Butternut Squash Risotto

Serves 4 Ⓥ

Fresh ingredients: butternut squash, onion, butter, Parmesan

1 medium butternut squash, peeled, de-seeded and cut
  into bite-sized cubes
3 tbsps Italian olive oil
1 large onion, peeled and finely chopped
4 juicy cloves garlic, peeled and well crushed
1 level tbsp dried Italian herb mix (see Tip)
300g risotto rice
850ml vegetable stock, hot
150ml Italian medium-dry wine
30g butter
100g Parmesan cheese, grated
salt and black pepper

I usually pre-cook the squash a little to soften
it – either by putting it in a bowl with 2 tbsps
water in the microwave for 5 minutes on high, or
by steaming over a saucepan of boiling water for
a similar time. I then drain it and pat it dry on
kitchen paper. If you don't want to do this, you
can just start from the next step but increase the
sautéing time on a low heat until the squash is soft.

Heat half the oil in a very large, high-sided
frying pan and, over a medium heat, sauté the
squash for about 5 minutes until golden and
cooked all the way through; remove to a dish and
reserve. Add the remaining oil and the onion to
the pan and sauté until softened and transparent –
about 8 minutes. Add the garlic and herbs and stir
for another minute or two.

Now add the rice to the pan and stir well to
coat the grains, then combine the stock and wine
in a pouring jug and add the mixture to the pan a
little at a time, waiting in between each addition
until the liquid is absorbed. When you have used
most of the liquid, try a little of the rice and see if
it is tender – if so, and the risotto looks nice and
creamy, you have added enough liquid. If not,
add more and cook a little longer, then stir in the
cooked squash.

To finish, stir in the butter and half the cheese,
and some black pepper and a little salt to taste,
and serve in a bowl or bowls, garnished with the
remaining cheese.

TIP

If you prefer, you can add 1–2 tbsps finely chopped
fresh herbs, such as sage, oregano or thyme. For good
makes of dried herbs and risotto rice, see A–Z.

Polenta with Peppers

Serves 4 **Ⓥ**

Fresh ingredients: Cheddar cheese, butter, basil

250g polenta cornmeal
50g Cheddar cheese, grated
30g butter
2–3 tbsps Italian olive oil
600g mixed sweet ready-roasted peppers in a jar, sliced
 (see Tip)
2–3 juicy cloves garlic, well crushed
1 dsp balsamic vinegar
large handful fresh basil
salt and black pepper

Bring 1.5 litres of lightly salted water to the boil in a large saucepan and sprinkle in the polenta, stirring all the time with a long-handled spoon. Reduce the heat and simmer very gently for 30 minutes, or until the polenta comes away from the sides of the pan when stirred, stirring from time to time (you don't want the polenta to stick on the bottom of the pan or burn).

Stir in the cheese and butter, then transfer the mixture to a shallow metal tin brushed with a little of the olive oil and leave to cool, by which time it should be firm enough to cut 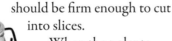 into slices.

When the polenta is cool, cut it into slices, brush it with some of the remaining olive oil and grill for a few minutes, until golden, turning once. Meanwhile, heat the rest of the olive oil in a non-stick frying pan and stir-fry the peppers and garlic for a few

minutes to colour, then stir in the vinegar, half the basil and a little salt and black pepper.

Serve the grilled polenta with the peppers and the remaining basil to garnish.

VARIATIONS

You can serve polenta with a mushroom ragout made using a mix of fresh (if you have any) and dried, wild mushrooms such as porcini. Just reconstitute these in a little water, which takes only 15 minutes or so. Meanwhile stir-fry any fresh mushrooms in olive oil, then simmer everything in a little stock, the mushroom soaking juice, red wine and herbs such as thyme and sage.

Instead of serving the polenta in slices, you can also use polenta meal to make a mash similar to mashed potato. Simply follow the initial process in this recipe, using half semi-skimmed milk and half water to simmer the polenta until it is cooked, then stir in a little extra milk with the cheese and butter to get a mash consistency.

TIP

For where to buy good peppers ready cooked for the storecupboard, see the A–Z. You could of course use fresh mixed peppers (4 large) if you have any – slice and stir-fry in the oil for 8–10 minutes or until soft and turning golden, then add the garlic, etc.

Ribollita

Serves 6 **V**

Fresh ingredients: celery, carrots, red onions, cabbage, parsley, ciabatta bread

2 x 400g cans cannellini beans, drained and rinsed (see Tip)
2 tbsps Italian olive oil
4 medium sticks celery, chopped
4 medium carrots, peeled and chopped
2 medium red onions, peeled and chopped
3 cloves garlic, peeled and well crushed
500g canned chopped Italian tomatoes
bunch flat-leaved parsley, de-stalked and chopped
250g cabbage, sliced
6 x 2cm-thick slices ciabatta bread
salt and black pepper

Leave half the beans whole and purée the other half in an electric blender, or mash thoroughly with a fork and set all the beans aside.

Heat the oil in a large saucepan on medium heat and add the celery, carrots, onions and garlic. Cook for 30 minutes on a low heat, stirring occasionally, then add the tomatoes, most of the parsley, the whole beans and the cabbage with enough boiling water to cover and some seasoning. Stir and bring to simmer, then cook for 20 minutes.

Stir the bean purée into the soup and add a little boiling water if the soup doesn't seem liquid enough. Check the seasoning and add some salt and pepper if necessary.

Drizzle the bread with olive oil and toast until golden, then arrange it on top of the soup and simmer for a minute or two so that the toast partially absorbs some liquid. Serve garnished with the remaining parsley

TIPS

If you have any dried cannellini beans and want to be more traditional, you can use these in the recipe. Follow the instructions for cooking 225g dried pulses in Chapter 2 and then purée half of them as above and continue with the recipe.

You can use vegetable stock instead of the water if you prefer.

Aubergine and Chickpea Stew with Couscous

Serves 4 **Ⓥ**

Fresh ingredients: aubergines, onion, mint, coriander, lemon

4 tbsps olive oil
2 medium aubergines (see Tip)
1 medium onion, peeled and finely chopped
2 juicy cloves garlic, peeled and crushed
1 tsp each ground coriander seed, cumin seed and paprika
1 tsp harissa paste
400g can chopped tomatoes
400g can chickpeas, drained and rinsed
300g couscous
600ml vegetable stock
grated rind of half a lemon
50g flaked toasted almonds
50g sultanas
good handful each fresh mint leaves and coriander leaves
salt and black pepper

Heat half the olive oil in a large, good-quality, lidded, non-stick frying pan. Top, tail and slice the aubergines into 1cm-thick slices, then into cubes and, over a medium-high heat, stir-fry the cubes until the aubergine is just soft and golden.

Note: they will absorb all the oil almost immediately, but keep your nerve, keep stirring and gradually they will cook without burning as they contain over 90 per cent water. Remove from the pan and set aside.

Add the remaining oil to the pan and sauté the onion over a medium-high heat, stirring from time to time, until soft, transparent and just turning golden. Add the garlic, ground spices and harissa paste and stir for a minute to release the aromas, then stir in the chopped tomatoes and the chickpeas, bring to simmer, put the lid on and simmer very gently for 30 minutes, stirring once or twice.

Meanwhile, put the couscous in a heatproof bowl and boil the stock, then pour over the couscous and leave to stand for 15 minutes. Stir in the lemon rind, almonds and sultanas and set aside, covered, to keep warm.

After the 30 minutes is up, stir the mint into the aubergine stew and cook for another 2 minutes, then stir in most of the coriander and season to taste. Serve the stew with the couscous and with a little fresh coriander sprinkled over.

TIP
You may need to cook the aubergine in two batches depending on the size of your pan and your own preference.

Slow-cooked Lamb with Sweet Potatoes

Serves 4

Fresh ingredients: onion, sweet potato, lamb, coriander or parsley

2–3 tbsps olive oil
600g lamb meat (see Tip), cut into large cubes
1 large onion, peeled and roughly chopped
2 cloves garlic, peeled and well crushed
1 large sweet potato, peeled and cut into bite-sized cubes
1 tsp each ground cumin, coriander seed and cinnamon
1 tbsp tomato purée
300ml lamb stock
150ml white wine
75g semi-dried dates, roughly chopped
salt and black pepper
300g bulghar wheat
handful fresh coriander, or flat-leaved parsley

Heat half the oil in a large flameproof casserole and add the lamb pieces; sauté over a high heat, turning as the sides brown, and when thoroughly coloured remove with a slotted spoon and reserve. Add the remaining oil to the pan with the onion, garlic and sweet potato, turn the heat down low and sauté for 15 minutes or until the onion is soft and transparent and the sweet potato semi-cooked.

Stir in the spices to release the aromas, then return the lamb to the pan with the tomato purée and stir well. Pour in the stock and wine, season well, then bring to a simmer, put the lid on and cook either in the oven at 160°C for 1½ hours or on the hob, very gently, for the same time, stirring halfway through.

Add the dates for the last 15 minutes of cooking, removing the lid if there seems to be too much liquid in the pan. Meanwhile, reconstitute the bulghar wheat according to the packet instructions – usually simply soak for 15 minutes in boiling water, or vegetable stock if preferred.

Serve the lamb stew with the bulghar wheat, garnished with the coriander or parsley.

TIP

You can use boned leg of lamb for this dish or, if you don't mind the extra fat and calories, you can use shoulder of lamb, which may produce a more succulent result, or neck fillet, which is also very good.

Cottage Pie with Lentils

Serves 4 **V**

Fresh ingredients: onion, carrots, celery, mushrooms, potatoes, butter, milk

2 tbsps light olive oil
1 large onion, peeled and finely chopped
1 clove garlic, peeled and finely chopped
2 large carrots, peeled and finely chopped
1 stick celery, peeled and finely chopped
150g dark-gilled mushrooms, finely chopped
2 x 400g cans brown lentils, drained and rinsed
400g can chopped tomatoes
1 tbsp soya sauce
200ml vegetable stock (see Tip)
800g floury potatoes, peeled and cubed (see Tip)
30g butter
30ml milk
salt and black pepper

Heat the oil in a large, non-stick frying pan and sauté the onion, garlic, carrot and celery over a medium-high heat, stirring frequently, until the vegetables are well softened – about 8 minutes. Stir in the mushrooms, lentils, tomatoes and soya sauce and combine well, cook for a minute, then stir in the stock. Bring to a simmer and cook for 10 minutes.

Meanwhile, boil the potatoes in lightly salted water for 15–20 minutes or until tender, drain well, add the butter, milk and some seasoning, and mash.

Spoon the lentil mixture into a family-sized pie dish then top with the mash. Bake for 20–25 minutes or until the top is golden, and serve.

Tips

You can make the vegetable stock a bit more concentrated than usual – use one typical cube in the 200ml water.

You can add other root vegetables to the potato for the mash – e.g. sweet potato or parsnip, or even celeriac. Just replace some of the potato with an equal weight of the alternative vegetables and cook them together in the boiling water.

You can use mixed pulses instead of all lentils, if you like – or different types of lentil. If you want to use dried lentils, add 250g lentils instead of the canned ones, add 200ml extra stock and simmer for 40 minutes rather than 10, or until the lentils are tender.

Chicken Satay with Peanut Sauce

Serves 4

Fresh ingredients: chicken, ginger, lime juice (optional), coriander leaves (optional)

1 small to medium whole chicken

FOR THE MARINADE:
1 tbsp soya sauce
1 tbsp runny honey
1tsp each ground turmeric, cumin and coriander
2 cloves garlic, well crushed
2cm piece fresh ginger, peeled and finely grated
juice of 1 lime, or 1 tbsp lime juice from bottle
1 tbsp groundnut oil

FOR THE SAUCE:
5 tbsp crunchy peanut butter
1 tsp Thai red curry paste
120ml coconut milk
2 tsps soft dark brown sugar
juice of half a lime, or 1 dsp lime juice from bottle
handful coriander leaves, chopped (optional)

Joint the chicken, cutting each breast and leg into two so that you have eight pieces and removing much of the skin. Pierce the chicken pieces several times each with a knife and put them in a shallow glass or china bowl.

Mix all the marinade ingredients together and stir into the chicken. Leave to marinate for at least 2 hours, or overnight if you can, turning occasionally.

When ready to cook, preheat the oven to 200°C.

To make the sauce, place all the ingredients, except the coriander, in a small pan and bring to a simmer. Cook for a couple of minutes until thickened, stirring occasionally, then set aside.

Transfer the chicken pieces to a roasting tray with the marinade and bake for about 30 minutes, turning occasionally, until golden and thoroughly cooked through. Serve with the peanut sauce (stirring in the fresh coriander if you are using it) and some Thai fragrant rice.

Beef and Red Lentil Main Course Soup

Serves 4

Fresh ingredients: onion, braising beef, carrot, swede

500g braising beef, cut into large bite-sized cubes
3 tbsps groundnut oil
1 large onion, peeled and roughly chopped
150g red lentils, dry weight
1 heaped tbsp tomato purée
1 tbsp Worcestershire sauce
800ml beef stock
1 level tbsp dried mixed herbs
250g carrots, peeled and roughly chopped
half a small swede, peeled and roughly chopped
salt and black pepper

Heat half the oil in a large flameproof casserole and brown the meat over a high heat. Remove the pieces from the pan as they brown; reserve. Add the remaining oil to the pan with the onion, and turn the heat down to medium-high. Sauté the onion, stirring occasionally, for 5 minutes to soften, then add the lentils and stir again. Add the tomato purée, Worcestershire sauce, stock, herbs and vegetables, stir everything and bring to a simmer. Put the lid on, and either cook in a low oven (160°C) for 2 hours, or gently simmer on the hob for a similar length of time.

Check once or twice that the soup isn't bubbling too fast and that there is sufficient liquid. (The soup at the end should be quite stew-like with plenty of liquid.) Before serving, add some salt and pepper to taste.

TIP

Serve with crusty bread.

Easy Chicken Tagine

Serves 4

Fresh ingredients: onion, chicken breast fillets, courgette, broad beans

1 medium onion, peeled and quartered
2 cloves garlic, peeled
heaped tsp each cumin, coriander and cinnamon
1 level tbsp harissa
2 tbsps olive oil
1 level tbsp tomato purée
level tsp each salt and black pepper
4 boneless chicken breast fillets, each cut into five
400g can chopped tomatoes
250ml vegetable stock
1 large courgette, topped, tailed and cut into 1cm slices
250g (podded weight) broad beans (see Tip)
2 tbsps sultanas
8 black olives, halved
4 slices preserved lemon

Put the onion, garlic, spices, harissa, half the olive oil, tomato purée and seasoning in an electric blender and blend for a minute until you have a paste. Heat the remaining olive oil in a large, lidded, non-stick frying pan and sauté the chicken pieces over a high heat for 2–3 minutes to brown lightly, then add the paste and stir for a minute to release the flavours. Add the tomatoes, stock, courgette and broad beans, stir well, bring to a simmer, turn the heat down low, put a lid on and cook for half an hour.

Add the sultanas, olives and preserved lemon slices and cook without the lid on for a further 10 minutes before serving.

TIPS

You can use a 300g can of broad beans, well drained, if you like, or you could use a can of flageolets, or 250g pre-cooked Egyptian brown beans (see A–Z).

Garnish the tagine with fresh coriander leaves if you have any, or with flat-leaved parsley. Serve it with couscous or bulghar wheat, or with flatbreads.

7 Salads and Side Dishes

You could be forgiven for thinking that it isn't possible to make much in the way of salads and side dishes from your storecupboard contents. However, while of course many salads need some fresh ingredients by their very definition, your stores can yield a variety of ingredients to make salads and sides much more interesting or substantial.

Main-course salads can also be produced from all kinds of larder items including pasta, rice or other grains, pulses and dried or preserved foods, just to give a few examples.

You will also want to dress your salads and sides in good style to add flavour, moisture and excitement – and this is where a good store can provide huge variety. Wonderful dressings can be made if you have a selection of oils and vinegars, while many storecupboard items such as nuts, seeds, capers, anchovies and so on can be sprinkled on as a finishing touch.

Lastly, I've come up with a few ideas for turning basic storecupboard items into almost-instant delicious treats – for example, there are various ways you can enliven and personalize a bought mayonnaise to turn it into a good dressing, dip or garnish.

Warm Green Lentil Salad

Serves 4 **V**

Fresh ingredients: shallots, lemon, herbs

200g dried green lentils
3 shallots, peeled and finely chopped
550ml vegetable stock
2 tbsps cold-pressed spicy olive oil
juice of 1 lemon
2 heaped tbsps fresh chopped herbs (see Tip)
salt and black pepper

Put the lentils in a saucepan with the shallots and stock, bring to a simmer and cook for 30 minutes or until the lentils are tender and almost all the stock is absorbed. Drain off any remaining stock.

Stir in the oil, lemon juice, herbs and seasoning. Allow to cool a little to serve warm, or can also be served cold.

Tips

I like to use fresh chopped mint and parsley, but you could also add coriander leaves or any other soft-leaved herb.

This salad is nice as part of a summer buffet, or is ideal with salmon, sea bass or other fish. It also goes well with bacon, ham, lamb and chicken, or you can serve it with brown rice as a vegetarian main course.

Chickpea and Red Pepper Salad

Serves 4 **V**

Fresh ingredients: tomatoes, mint, coriander leaves

400g can chickpeas, drained and rinsed
3 juicy, ripe but still firm tomatoes, roughly chopped
300g jar roasted peppers, drained and sliced
1 tbsp each chopped mint and coriander leaves
3 tbsps fruity olive oil
1 tbsp balsamic vinegar
1 tsp Dijon mustard
1 level tsp ready-minced chilli
salt and black pepper

Tip the chickpeas, tomatoes and peppers into a serving bowl with the herbs and stir to combine.

In a bowl, mix together the olive oil, vinegar, mustard, chilli and seasoning, then stir this dressing into the chickpea mix.

Tip

This salad goes well with sharp cheeses, such as feta, with tuna fish and as part of a buffet.

Brown Lentil, Rice and Vegetable Salad

Serves 4–6 Ⓥ

Fresh ingredients: squash or pumpkin, broccoli, tomatoes, mint, parsley

2 tbsps soya sauce
2 tbsps balsamic vinegar
2 tbsps groundnut oil
1 tbsp sesame seed oil
1 level dsp chopped stem ginger
150g brown lentils (see Tip)
150g brown rice
400g orange-fleshed squash or pumpkin (about 1 small butternut), peeled, de-seeded and chopped into small cubes
250g small broccoli florets
2 large tomatoes, chopped
1 tbsp sundried tomatoes, chopped
1 tbsp each fresh mint and parsley, chopped

In a bowl or blender, combine the first five ingredients, adding a little salt if you feel it needs it, but the soya sauce is quite salty. Set aside.

Cook the lentils and rice together in 750ml boiling water until tender – about 25 minutes – adding extra boiling water if the pan begins to dry out. If you have a steamer, add the squash and broccoli to that and cook over the lentil mix until tender. When the lentils and rice are cooked (by which time all the liquid should have been absorbed but the grains should still be slightly moist), season lightly and tip into a large bowl.

When the lentils are cooled to just warm, stir in the cooked vegetables, the tomatoes, herbs and dressing and combine well.

TIPS

You can use Puy lentils for a finer flavour, or you can even use green lentils.

Classic Three Bean Salad

Serves 4 Ⓥ

Fresh ingredients: green beans, spring onions, tomatoes, flat-leaf parsley

125g green beans, halved
1 large clove juicy garlic, peeled
1 quantity Basic Salad Dressing (see page 159)
400g can cannellini or red kidney beans, drained and rinsed
400g can flageolet or black-eyed beans, drained and rinsed
6 spring onions, chopped
2 large, ripe tomatoes
4 tbsps chopped flat-leaf parsley

Lightly steam the beans for 2–3 minutes until *al dente*, drain and refresh under cold running water, then pat dry.

Put the garlic in a mortar if you have one, and crush it well, gradually adding the salad dressing and mixing in. Otherwise, crush the garlic with the flat side of a heavy knife on a chopping board and scrape it all into a mixing bowl to combine with the dressing.

Tip the beans into a bowl with the spring onions and toss with the dressing. Halve, de-seed and roughly chop the tomatoes and add them to the bowl with the parsley.

TIPS

You can add 150g torn buffalo Mozzarella to the salad if you have any to make a good lunch.

A teaspoon of mild curry powder or smoked paprika added to the dressing will give the salad a spicier kick.

Turkish Bean Salad

Serves 4 Ⓥ

Fresh ingredients: red onion, lettuce, lemon, parsley

400g can butter or cannellini beans, drained and rinsed
1 medium red onion, peeled and thinly sliced
2 roast sweet peppers from a jar, drained and roughly
   chopped
2 little gem heads, or 1 cos lettuce
2 tbsps olive oil
juice of half a lemon
salt and black pepper
2 tsps lightly crushed coriander seeds
handful fresh flat-leaved parsley, chopped

Tip the beans, onion and peppers into a serving bowl. Prepare the lettuce, discarding any browning or poor-quality outside leaves, and cut the heart into slices. Add to the bowl.

Combine the olive oil, lemon juice, seasoning and coriander seeds in a bowl and spoon over the salad, mixing lightly, then garnish with parsley to serve.

TIP

This bean salad is nice as part of a buffet, or can be used as a starter or as a side dish to go with lamb or chicken.

Spinach with Raisins

Serves 4 **Ⓥ**

Fresh ingredients: spinach, spring onions

6 spring onions, chopped
4 tbsps raisins
1kg fresh tender spinach leaves
4 tbsps toasted pine nuts (see Tip)
2 tbsps olive oil
salt and black pepper

Heat the oil in a large, non-stick frying pan and stir-fry the spring onion and raisins for a few minutes to plump up the raisins and colour the onion. Add the spinach and stir until it is wilted – this should take a few minutes. Add the pine nuts and stir again, season to taste, stir and serve.

TIP

If you have no toasted pine nuts you can toast untoasted nuts in the dry frying pan for a few minutes, removing them from the pan before adding the oil.

Noodle Salad with Broccoli

Serves 4

Fresh ingredients: broccoli, prawns, red pepper, limes

4 x 50g nests wholewheat noodles (see Tip)
1 tbsp groundnut oil
200g broccoli, cut into small florets
1 fresh red pepper, de-seeded and cut into thin strips
4 tbsps ketjap manis (see Tip)
1 tsp ready-chopped chilli
2 tsps ready-minced garlic
2 tsps ready-minced ginger
juice of 2 limes
100g small peeled prawns

Cook the noodles in lightly salted boiling water for 3–4 minutes or according to packet instructions, then drain. Meanwhile, heat the oil in a non-stick frying pan and stir-fry the broccoli and pepper for 3 minutes over a high heat or until the vegetables are *al dente* and lightly coloured.

Combine the ketjap manis, chilli, garlic, ginger and lime juice in a bowl. When the noodles are ready, tip them into a serving bowl or bowls and stir in the vegetables, prawns and dressing before serving.

TIPS

If you can't find the wholewheat noodle nests, you can use ordinary egg-thread noodles or soba noodles.

Ketjap manis is a delicious, thick, soya-type sauce (see A–Z).

This noodle salad is good as part of a buffet or can be used as a side dish with any Chinese, Japanese or Thai meat, poultry or fish recipe.

Chilli and Coriander Sambal

Serves 4

Fresh ingredients: green pepper, green chilli, lime

1 green pepper, de-seeded and chopped
1 green chilli, de-seeded
1 tsp ready-minced ginger
2 juicy cloves garlic, peeled
3 tbsps ready-made coriander pesto (see Tip)
1 tsp sweet chilli dipping sauce
1 dsp white wine vinegar
juice of 1 lime

Put all the ingredients into an electric blender and whizz until you have a thick paste. It will keep in a lidded container in the fridge for a few days.

TIPS

It's vital that you use a good-quality pesto in this dish – Sacla is widely available and tastes good. You can add a handful of fresh coriander to the blender if you have any and if you like you can of course use fresh ginger – 1 small knob, peeled.

The sambal is nice served with grilled salmon or chicken.

8 Preserves, Chutneys, Sauces and Pastes

In our busy lives it is sometimes important to take time to relax at home. One of the best ways I know of doing this is to make your own preserves from seasonal and local produce – perhaps even from your own garden. Making your own is also hugely satisfying – and the end result should be superior to much more expensive similar products in the shops.

Throughout the seasons you can find different produce to turn into preserves for storing: berry jams in summer, citrus marmalades in winter, apple or pear chutney in autumn, for example.

For this chapter I have mainly chosen ingredients that you may find, if not in your own garden, then in a neighbour's or at the local market. For example, damsons are a reliable tree fruit and a damson tree is still not an uncommon site in suburban and country gardens and old orchards. Damsons, and indeed other tree fruits such as plums and apples, tend to be in glut every other year – so if you have a glut, preserve or bottle them!

Many jam and preserve recipes contain inordinate amounts of sugar. I try to use as little sugar as possible, but one has to be careful about low-sugar preserves and use them up within weeks or a couple of months, as their keeping power is reduced. If a recipe is reduced-sugar I will advise you about storage in the tips that accompany each recipe.

Jams and other preserves

Here are some general guidelines about making jam, marmalade and preserves which are appropriate for most of the recipes in this chapter. Do read these notes before trying out any recipe.

Saving jars all year round

To save having to buy new jars (which are quite expensive), plan ahead and save old jam and other jars rather than putting them out for recycling. But don't save cracked or chipped jars. It will help if you have a variety of different sizes. Straight-sided jars are easier to fill than those with a neck that narrows off (though the latter may look prettier!).

Some glass jars do still smell of the previous contents even after thorough washing – I find jars that have contained pickles to be among the worst for this. When you save a jar, wash it and dry it thoroughly and store it without a lid. You can save lids, but these are often not too good to look at. Instead you can buy new lids, or, for jam- and chutney-making, just use greaseproof circles, cellophane and rubber bands (in which case the preserves may have a shorter shelf-life as you won't have an airtight seal).

If you do have to buy jars, there is a section on containers, and where to get them, in the A–Z.

Plan ahead

Once you've decided you're going to make your own preserve, you need to set aside enough time to do the job – a Sunday afternoon is ideal, especially if it's raining! You need, of course, to have your fruit in good condition, to have done any pre-prep (e.g. soaking) and to have all the ingredients to hand, so read the recipe properly several days before you begin.

You also need to decide how much you want to make and have enough clean, sterilized pots available (see below), with accessories. And of course you need enough fruit (or whatever you are using) to make the required number of pots. (A tip – if you do make too much you can always give surplus away as presents, or swap with neighbours.)

Before you begin, you need to have items such as your preserving pan, oven gloves, long-handled spoons (wooden) and teaspoons ready, some cold saucers to test set (see below), some kitchen paper to set the jars on before filling, a funnel, and all your labels, lids, tops, etc.

Strawberry Conserve

I gave up making strawberry jam several years ago as it was never that successful – either it wouldn't set until boiled to a nasty dark colour, or it didn't keep for more than a couple of weeks, or it tasted far too sweet – and that includes when I used pectin-enriched sugar.

But one of the younger members of the local WI group gave me a new recipe last year which she swore was wonderful, and so I gave it one last go. It was the absolute best strawberry jam I have ever tasted, and it looks superb with whole fruits and a lovely, true, light strawberry-red colour. The set is very soft and I will admit that to keep the last couple of pots in good order late into the year, I put them in the fridge. Nearly a year later, the last little pot left is still in good condition. The only amazement is that there is any left at all. Oh, and it is too posh to call jam, so I shall call it conserve.

Anyway, here is the recipe.

Makes about 6 x 400ml pots

Fresh ingredients: strawberries, lemon

2kg ripe but not over-ripe strawberries (see Tip)
1.5kg preserving sugar with added pectin
1 lemon

Begin the night, or at least 6 hours, before you want to make the jam. Hull the strawberries and layer them in a large bowl with the sugar in between the layers. Cover and leave overnight or for at least 6 hours.

Next morning, or at least 6 hours later, you'll find that the sugar has part-dissolved and you have a red juice in the bowl as well as some undissolved sugar and the strawberries. Tip the contents of the bowl into your preserving pan and heat very gently, without stirring, until all the sugar is dissolved. This shouldn't take more than 5–6 minutes.

Squeeze the lemon and add the juice, bring to the boil and boil for 8 minutes, then test for set (see page 171). If you don't get a set, repeat the boiling in 2-minute intervals until you do. Once you have a light set, leave to cool for 15 minutes, stir to distribute the fruit, then follow the procedure on page 172 for potting and storing.

TIP

Most of the strawberries for sale in the UK are Elsanto, which are pretty to look at but not the most flavoursome. See if you can find other varieties in local markets or greengrocers – or buy some plants for the patio or borders next year.

Rhubarb and Ginger Jam

I always have tons of rhubarb in the kitchen garden and can't eat enough to use it all up fresh, so I freeze some and like to use surplus for either jam or chutney.

Makes about 6 x 400ml pots

Fresh ingredients: rhubarb, ginger, lemon

2kg rhubarb
2kg preserving sugar
finger-length piece of fresh ginger
1 lemon

This jam should also be started several hours before you intend to boil it up, if possible. Trim the rhubarb and wash as necessary, wipe dry and cut into 2cm chunks, then layer in a large bowl with the sugar. Leave for several hours or even overnight, by which time the sugar will have partially dissolved.

Tip the rhubarb mix into your preserving pan. Peel the piece of ginger, bash it a little with a rolling pin or cleaver, and put it in a muslin bag – preferably one with a long handle which you can tie to the handle of the pan. Juice the lemon and add the juice to the pan with the ginger, then heat gently until all the sugar is dissolved.

Now boil rapidly for 15 minutes, then test for set (see page 171) and repeat, if necessary, testing every few minutes until you do have a set. Remove the ginger in the muslin, leave to cool for 15 minutes then follow the steps for potting up, as described on page 172.

TIP

Some recipes tell you to add finely chopped mixed peel to the jam when you add the ginger and juice – if you want to try that, add about 30g, but I haven't tried it myself.

Quince Jelly

We are lucky enough to have our own quince tree, which has beautiful blossom in spring, interesting leaves and the most gorgeous fruit most years. Quinces are becoming more popular again, I think. They look a bit like pears with a furry skin, are absolutely as hard as bullets when raw but turn into delicious, tangy fruit when cooked. Quince jelly is a lovely accompaniment to meats.

The recipe here is based on Eliza Acton's old one – she is a bit vague with amounts, but this seems to work well enough.

Makes about 6 x 400ml pots
Fresh ingredients: quinces, lemon

2kg quinces
1 lemon
approx. 1kg sugar

Peel and quarter the quinces, but don't remove the pips or cores. Straight away (so they don't discolour) put them in a pan with 2 litres of water, bring to the boil and simmer gently, covered, until tender. This takes varying lengths of time depending on the hardness of the quinces, but mine fresh off the tree usually take only about an hour, though I have heard reports of its taking a couple of hours or more. What you want is a pretty, reddish-tinged juice by the time you've finished simmering. When tender, leave the quinces in the liquid for several hours or overnight, then strain the whole lot through a muslin (jelly) bag into a large bowl for 12 hours, covering to protect against flies, etc. Don't squeeze the fruit or the juice for the jelly will be cloudy and you want it clear.

When ready, pour the juice into a measuring jug and have ready 350g sugar for each half litre of juice.

Add the sugar to the juice in a preserving pan with the juice of the lemon and dissolve over gentle heat, then boil rapidly for 10 minutes before testing for setting point (see page 171). If the jelly isn't set, continue to boil and test every couple of minutes until it is, then, using thick, heatproof gloves, pour the jelly into prepared sterilized pots (see page 172).

Seville Orange Marmalade

I'm not a marmalade-maker, but my friend David makes excellent Seville orange marmalade each January (he rightly says that Sevilles are the only kind of orange worth trying to make marmalade with, and they are in season only in winter) and is kind enough to give me a pot or two. This is his recipe.

Makes about 6 x 400ml pots
Fresh ingredients: Seville oranges, lemon

1kg Seville oranges, preferably organic or thoroughly washed
1 lemon
2kg preserving sugar

Remove the peel from the oranges and cut it into thin strips. Halve the oranges and squeeze the juice into a bowl. Chop up any remaining orange flesh and separate the pith – put it into a muslin bag with the orange pips.

Place the peel, strained juice, pulp and 2 litres of water into your preserving pan with the muslin containing the pips and any pith, and simmer gently for 2 hours or until the peel is tender.

Remove the muslin bag and leave the marmalade to cool a little, then squeeze the lemon and add its juice to the pan. Now squeeze the muslin bag over the pan too, as the pips and pith contain valuable pectin to help the marmalade set.

Add the sugar to the pan and dissolve it slowly over a gentle heat. When it is fully dissolved, bring the pan to the boil and boil rapidly until the setting point is reached (see page 171), which can happen from around 15 minutes on. Pot up as on page 172.

Redcurrant Jelly

I have two redcurrant bushes, but I never get much fruit as the birds always get it first – so I go to the farm shop and do 'pick your own'! I think the birds deserve their fruit for helping to keep my greenfly and snails at bay. So I don't make much redcurrant jelly, but obviously if you want more, just double the quantities.

Makes about 6 x 150ml pots
Fresh ingredients: redcurrants

1kg redcurrants on the stalk
sugar

Destalk the redcurrants with a fork. Put the redcurrants into a pan and cover with water. Bring to the boil and cook until the fruit is pulpy, then pour into a jelly bag (see previous recipe) and strain for 12 hours. Measure the juice, pour into a preserving pan and add 200g sugar for every 250ml juice you have.

Dissolve the sugar in the juice over a low heat. When thoroughly dissolved bring to a rapid boil and boil for 5 minutes. Test for a set (see page 171) and repeat if setting point isn't reached, boiling for a further 1–2 minutes.

When the jelly has reached setting point, pour it into small (about 150ml) pots and proceed as explained on page 172.

Tandoori Mix

1 tsp each ground cumin, coriander and turmeric
½ tsp hot ground chilli
2 tsps ground sweet paprika

Mix all the ingredients together and store.

TIP

When you come to make the tandoori, add 1 tsp each of ready-chopped garlic and ginger and a little salt, and mix with a little natural yogurt and lemon juice to coat chicken, fish, etc., before grilling or baking.

All-purpose Medium-hot 'Curry' Blend

30g cumin seeds
30g coriander seeds
10g each of poppy seeds, mustard seeds, black peppercorns, fenugreek seeds
2 hot dried chillies
30g ground turmeric
10g ground dried ginger

Toast the whole spices as for Garam Masala, allow to cool, then grind in an electric blender, combine with the turmeric and ginger and store in an airtight opaque container in a cool, dry, dark place.

TIPS

Use 1–2 tbsps, depending on heat required, in a main dish for four people.

Use extra chilli for more heat. Fry the blend in oil in the pan before adding the rest of the ingredients – or, if the recipe requires you to sauté onions, the spice mix can be added when the onions are nearly ready and stirred until you can smell the aromas.

Jamaican Jerk Seasoning

1 heaped tbsp cayenne pepper
1 tbsp dried thyme
1 level tbsp sugar
1 heaped tsp ground allspice
1 heaped tsp sweet paprika
1 tsp black pepper
1 tsp salt
1 tsp dried ground sage
1 level tsp ground cinnamon
½ tsp ground nutmeg

Combine all ingredients together well and store in an airtight jar for a month or two.

TIPS

To use, rub the blend into meat, etc., before grilling or roasting. Very lean cuts of meat or chicken should be tossed in a little groundnut or other vegetable oil before you rub in the spice.

There are several different recipes for Jamaican Jerk seasoning. This one is medium hot. You can use more cayenne to taste, and you can substitute ground chilli for the cayenne, which is broadly the same.

Some recipes use more allspice, and others add onion and/or garlic powder, but I don't stock these in my larder. Instead, I might add some lazy garlic purée to the mix just before coating my meat.

Ras el Hanout 1

This spice mix varies tremendously in what is included, but a fairly typical, and pleasant, version is:

5g aniseeds
10g each of fennel seeds, allspice, green cardamom
   seeds, black peppercorns
2cm cinnamon stick
10g each of coriander seeds, dried chilli, ground galangal

Grind the whole spices, add the galangal and store in an airtight tin.

Ras el Hanout 2

A slightly more complicated version:

1 cinnamon stick, roughly broken
1 tsp cloves
1 dsp each of whole coriander seeds, cumin seeds,
   fenugreek, fennel seeds, mustard seeds
handful dried Damascan rose petals (available online or at
   Moroccan food stores)

Toast all the seeds over a low heat in a non-stick frying pan until the seeds begin to make a popping noise. Stir them around for a minute, still popping. Grind them with the rose petals in a coffee-grinder or pestle and mortar while still warm.

Will store for several weeks.

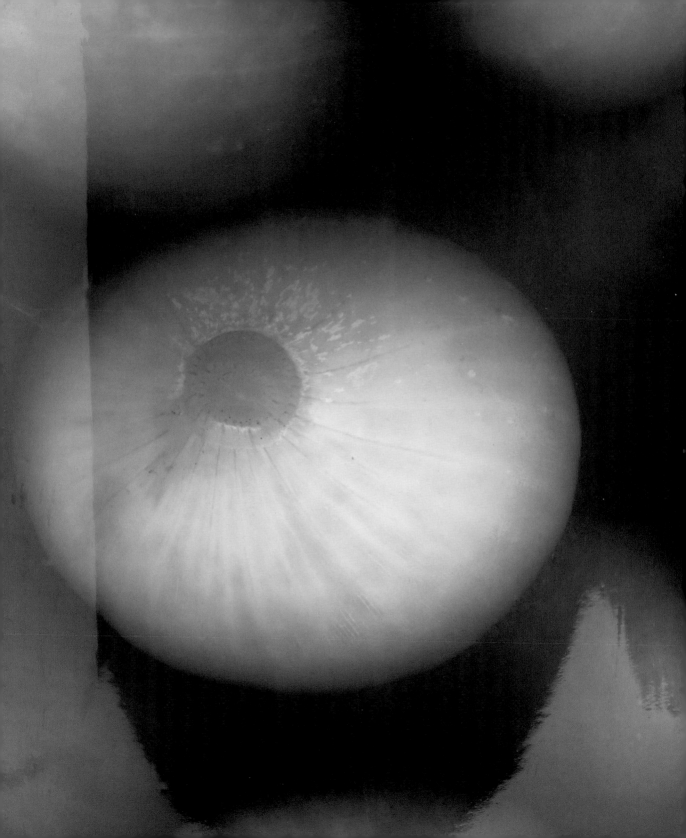

9 Bottling, Drying and Pickling

If you aren't so keen on jams you can use up a glut of fruits or certain vegetables around the seasons: bottled plums, pears, cherries, apricots, beetroot, red cabbage, artichokes, tomatoes, pickled onions, piccalilli, can all be successfully made at home.

Unlike jams and marmalades, bottled fruits and sauces are usually sterilized after the containers are filled to help them last longer. (You should also use pre-sterilized jars before filling them.) If you don't do this they will usually last up to a few weeks, but shouldn't be considered a long-store item and are best kept in a very cool place or in the fridge. Preserving in vinegar (savoury items) or alcohol (sweet items) is a good way to increase shelf-life, and produce covered in oil will also keep quite well – but all are best kept somewhere cool and dark.

Here is the general method for sterilizing filled containers. For information on where to buy sterilizing equipment, see the A–Z.

To sterilize in boiling water

Put the filled jars or bottles in a deep pan into which you have set a metal or wooden rack. Make sure they don't touch each other or the sides of the container or the bottom of the pan, or they will crack. Screw tops should be in place but not fully tight.

Add enough warm water to come up to the bottom of the screw tops and then gradually heat the water slowly until you see small bubbles rising from the base of the pan – a bare simmer. Maintain this for 30 minutes then use tongs to remove the bottles, and tighten the screw tops to seal.

To sterilize in the oven

After filling, put the lids on but don't fully tighten them. Put a few layers of newspaper or kitchen paper on a roasting tray and stand the jars on it, keeping them a few inches apart. Put the tray in the oven at 140°C and leave for 45 minutes.

Remove from the oven and tighten the lids to seal.

Globe Artichokes in Lemon Oil

Makes 3 x 400ml jars

Fresh ingredients: small globe artichokes, lemons

2kg baby globe artichokes
2 organic lemons, zested and squeezed
200ml white wine vinegar
approx. 400ml light olive oil
salt and black pepper

Prepare the artichokes by stripping off the tough outer leaves, using a sharp vegetable knife. Eventually you will come to the tender central section of the artichoke. Leaving a few centimetres of stalk on the vegetable, cut each one lengthways into quarters and dip each into the lemon juice so that they don't discolour.

Put 1 litre of water into a large saucepan and bring to the boil, add half the vinegar and the artichoke hearts and bring back to the boil. Turn the heat down and simmer for 12–15 minutes or until when poked with a sharp knife the artichokes are tender. Drain thoroughly, tip them into a bowl and combine with a little olive oil and some seasoning.

Now heat the grill and put the artichokes directly on to the base of the grill pan, then cook for a few minutes, turning once to colour each side. While this is happening, heat the remaining vinegar and lemon juice with 1 tbsp of the zest in a muslin bag in a small saucepan until just beginning to bubble, then remove from the heat. In another pan heat the oil until hot.

Pack the artichokes into sterilized jars (see page 170), pour over the hot vinegar and lemon mixture, then top up with oil to cover. Seal while warm, then allow to cool and put the lids on.

TIPS

The jars are best kept in a very cool place or in the fridge and the artichokes used up within 2 weeks as they don't go through the final, filled sterilizing process outlined on page 189.

These are ideal with French dressing and served as part of a buffet, or in a salad with baby broad beans or crisp salad leaves.

Pickled Onions

Makes about 1kg

Fresh ingredients: small pickling onions

1kg small pickling onions (see Tip), peeled
1 tbsp sea salt
1 litre malt vinegar
1 tsp dried chilli flakes
175g granulated sugar

Start the day before you want to complete the pickling by putting the onions and salt in a large bowl and mixing them together thoroughly, then cover the bowl and leave the onions for up to 12 hours or overnight.

When this time is up, rinse the onions in cold water and pat them dry gently using kitchen paper, then put the onions into two 500ml sterilized jars (see page 170).

Put the vinegar, chilli flakes and sugar into a pan and slowly bring to the boil to dissolve the sugar, stirring from time to time, then pour this mixture over the onions to cover them completely, and seal the jars. Allow the onions to mature for at least a couple of weeks before eating.

then put the onions into two 500ml sterilized jars (see page 170).

TIPS

You can use round pickling onions, widely available in the autumn, or shallots. Pickled onions go well with strong cheese, ham and cold meats.

You can use a similar recipe for sliced red cabbage – leave it overnight with the salt, drain and pack it into your jars, then completely cover it with vinegar which you have already brought to the boil with some peppercorns, a piece of ginger and a whole dried chilli in a muslin bag, then allowed to cool.

Pickled beetroot is similarly easy to do – just cook, peel and slice small beetroots, pack them into sterilized jars and completely cover them with vinegar which you have already brought to a boil with some peppercorns, cloves and allspice in a muslin bag, then allowed to cool.

Bottled Passata

Makes 1 litre

Fresh ingredients: ripe tomatoes

2kg clean tomatoes
1 tbsp caster sugar
salt

Cut the tomatoes in half and put them in a large saucepan with a spoonful or two of water, bring to a simmer and cook gently, covered, for 20 minutes or until soft. Allow to cool a little and press through a sieve to remove the skins and pips, returning the sieved tomato to a clean saucepan.

Add a spoonful of caster sugar and a little salt if you like, or leave as they are. Bring to the boil then immediately pour into sterilized preserving jars and put the lids on.

This will last for up to 4 weeks in a cool, dark place.

TIPS

Depending on how thick you want your tomato liquid, you can bottle as is for a thick passata or add extra water after sieving and before boiling to make a thinner mixture or to make tomato 'juice'.

For a slightly rougher purée which avoids the need to press the tomatoes through a sieve (not that this takes long really), you can simply allow the cooked tomatoes to cool then blend them in an electric blender, skins and all, then return them to the pan and continue as above.

You can make your own tomato paste by adding chopped sundried tomatoes, blended in an electric blender, to the tomato mix and simmering, uncovered, until the mix reduces to a paste. Spoon into jars as above.

An easy way to preserve tomatoes: pack cherry tomatoes, peeled garlic cloves and basil leaves into preserving jars, put them in a low oven for 45 minutes and then seal the jars immediately. They will store for a few months and are good with cold meats or stirred into pasta.

Bottled Pears 1

For this recipe I am indebted to Fiona Neville, a smallholder who lives in Cambridgeshire and writes an interesting blog at www. cottagesmallholder.com She calls these Belgian Pears and says they are a delicious dessert and taste as if they contain alcohol. I haven't tried them yet but will be doing so in the autumn when, hopefully, I will have some pears to pick!

Makes 2kg

Fresh ingredients: pears

2kg firm pears (see Tip)
500g granulated sugar
150ml white wine vinegar

Wash and peel the pears but leave the stalks on. Melt the sugar in the vinegar and any pear juice in a large, heavy-bottomed saucepan over a low heat, then add the pears and simmer very gently (as low as you can get), with a tight-fitting lid on, for 3 hours.

Remove the lid and simmer for a further 3 hours with the lid off.

Put into sterilized jars and seal (see page 170).

TIPS

Firm pears such as Conference are best – soft pears don't work so well.

You could add flavourings such as cinnamon or a little nutmeg, but Fiona says you don't need anything extra really.

Mrs Beeton's Bottled Pears 2

I have left in a précised version of Mrs Beeton's instructions for sterilizing the filled bottles, as although I have already given you a modern version of this process (see page 189), I think this is fascinating. Follow whichever method you prefer – mine or hers! I expect most of us have some spare hay wisps around, should we ever need them!

Makes 2kg
Fresh ingredients: pears

2kg pears (see Tip)
225g sugar

Peel, halve and core the pears and pack them into sterilized wide-neck 1-litre glass preserving jars. Sprinkle over the sugar.

Put the lids on the jars, then untwist them a little and place the jars in a large pan of cold water up to their necks, with small hay wisps (!! you could use teatowels) round them to prevent the bottles from knocking together (also put the jars on a thick wodge of paper or material, as they may crack otherwise).

Heat the water gradually to boiling and let it simmer gently until the fruit in the bottles is reduced by nearly a third – about 1½ hours.

Turn off the heat and let the bottles stand in the water until it is perfectly cold, then take them out and tighten the lids. Store in a dry place.

Bottled Plums

Makes 2kg
Fresh ingredients: plums

2kg just-ripe, tasty, unbruised plums – e.g. Victoria
500g sugar

First make a syrup by putting the sugar and a litre of water in a heavy-bottomed pan and dissolving the sugar over a low heat, stirring occasionally. Then bring the liquid to the boil and simmer for a few minutes; allow to cool.

Pack the fruit into sterilized jars (see page 170), pour on the syrup to fill the jars and sterilize, filled, as described on page 189.

Peaches in Brandy

Makes 2kg

Fresh ingredients: peaches

2kg fresh, just-ripe whole peaches
1kg sugar
400ml good-quality brandy

Put the peaches into boiling water in a pan for a minute, then remove and peel them. Put them in a china bowl with the sugar (see Tip), cover and leave overnight, by which time most of the sugar should have dissolved.

Transfer everything to a preserving pan and bring it slowly to a simmer so that the remaining sugar dissolves. Once it has dissolved, remove the peaches from the pan with a slotted spoon and pack them into sterilized jars.

Add the brandy to the pan, stir and bring to a boil with the peach syrup, then pour this mixture over the peaches to cover completely, and seal.

TIP

If you prefer, you can halve and stone the peaches before covering them with the sugar.

Drying Your Own Fruits and Vegetables

You can dry a wide variety of produce which will store well for several weeks.

Oven-drying is a good method of preserving some types of fruits and vegetables, including tomatoes, mushrooms, apricots and apples. They can then be added to salads, soups, cereals, desserts or casseroles to lend flavour, colour or texture. You may lose much of the fresh colour of paler or bright fruits or vegetables – those you buy in the shops keep their colour because they are treated with chemicals. The flavour of yours will be just as good, though.

All you need to do is prepare the produce:

Apples: peel, core and cut into rings.

Pears: peel, core and cut into slices.

Apricots: halve, remove stone.

Plums: halve, remove stone.

Tomatoes: cut into quarters (if there is any green, hard bit around the stalk end, remove this by cutting into the tomato with a sharp knife first).

Mushrooms: clean with a damp piece of kitchen paper, gently. Cut larger mushrooms into slices, leave small mushrooms whole or just halved.

Now arrange the produce in a single layer on a baking tray – a perforated pizza tray is ideal for firm fruits such as apples and pears. Put the tray in a very low oven (120°C) or the bottom, cool oven of an Aga and leave for several hours until completely dry. If using an ordinary oven you can increase the heat to 130°C after 2 hours and then 140°C for the last hour or until the drying process is complete.

Spread the produce out on kitchen paper to cool, covered with a dry teatowel, in a dry and dark place for a couple of hours, turning once. Then store in an opaque, airtight container in a cool, dry place and use within a few weeks. Check regularly to make sure they look OK.

TIP

You can dip apples and pears into lemon juice before drying, which may help to preserve a paler shade. I have also heard it recommended that you can dip them into salted water (1 tbsp salt to 1 litre water) for a similar effect, but I haven't tried it myself.

Drying Your Own Herbs and Spices

Some herbs, particularly the more robust leaves, dry quite well and retain much of their flavour – indeed, the intenseness of some (including rosemary and thyme) actually seems to be enhanced by the drying process.

Sage and rosemary: If I am in a hurry I simply cut branches off the herb bushes, tie them together in smallish bundles and hang them from the ceiling or even cupboard doors in a dry, warm room, where they seem to dry happily over a period of a few days. They can be left where they are to use as you want over the weeks ahead, or the leaves can be removed and put into an airtight container in a dark place.

Otherwise you could remove the leaves from the stalks and dry them in a low oven, as with fruit (above), then store them in an airtight container in a dark place.

Thyme, oregano and marjoram: Remove the leaves from the stalks with a fork or your clean fingernails and leave them in a shallow dish in a warm room. Stir with a fork occasionally until dried, then decant into an airtight container.

Parsley, basil and coriander leaves: I don't bother trying to dry these as they lose most of their flavour. I would rather preserve them in oil or keep a couple of pots on the windowsill through the winter. You can sow basil and coriander at almost any time of year, while parsley will keep going outdoors all year round.

Mint: This can be dried and is a little more successful. De-stalk and dry the leaves in a very low oven on a baking sheet for about 1½ hours or until dry. Crush with a rolling pin or leave whole, then store in an airtight container in a dry, dark place.

Chillies: I love to grow chillies and whole ones dry very successfully. I bring them into the house, put them in a shallow dish in the kitchen and over a period of a week or so they dry out and retain their colour. You can leave them where they are, or store them in an airtight container in a dry, dark place. You can use them as they are or crumble them into sauces, etc., or remove the seeds and then use them. You can also preserve your fresh chillies in oil (see Basil in Olive Oil, page 193).

10 Puddings, Cakes, Breads and Biscuits

Few of us are keen home bakers any more, which is sad. Yes, I do know that those of us who regularly eat a lot of baked goods may find our waistlines increasing at an alarming rate – but if you are a very active person, and/or are trying to feed hungry, skinny, sport-mad teenagers and the like, then the occasional home-made pudding or cake, or some cookies for a packed lunch, is a wonder.

Baking is not actually difficult, but it is more of an exact science than many other types of cooking, as the correct amounts of ingredients such as flour, fat, sugar and, perhaps, raising agent, synergize to make a correct mix for the finished product.

But anyone can bake – particularly if you start off with simple things such as flapjacks or a fruit crumble. You can then progress to other delights, such as fruit cake and old-fashioned wholesome puddings, updated as necessary. Your larder is a veritable treasure trove of potential baking ingredients.

Baking is a real home-enhancing thing to do – and it is good for your soul, too. Lastly, I've never known a friend, relative or neighbour who doesn't appreciate a gift of a lovingly home-made cake or basket of biscuits.

Flapjacks

Makes 8

Fresh ingredient: apple juice (optional)

150ml groundnut oil
150ml apple juice – either fresh or longlife
100g oatmeal (fine)
150g rolled oats
25g sunflower seeds
50g ready-to-eat dried apricots, chopped
a pinch of salt

Combine all the ingredients in a mixing bowl, then spoon into a shallow 18cm-square baking tin, press down well and smooth the top until even.

Bake at 190°C until golden – about 20–25 minutes – then mark into eight pieces and allow to cool before removing from the tin and cutting.

Mixed Grain Bread

Makes a 1kg loaf or 2 small loaves

450g fine oatmeal (oatflour)
100g wholemeal bread flour
50g soya flour
1 sachet easy-blend yeast
1 tsp sea salt
I level tbsp soft brown sugar
1 tbsp groundnut oil
400ml warm water

Mix together the flours with the yeast, salt and sugar in a mixing bowl; add the oil and water and combine thoroughly until you have a soft ball of dough.

On a lightly floured surface, knead the dough thoroughly for 10 minutes or until it is elastic and smooth. If making two small loaves, divide the mix into two.

Leave the dough in a lightly oiled 1kg loaf tin (or two 500g loaf tins), covered with a damp teatowel, in a warm place for about 40 minutes or until well risen.

Heat the oven to 190°C and bake the loaves for 50 minutes or until they sound hollow when the base is tapped. Turn out on to a rack and allow to cool.

TIP

You can make an ordinary wholemeal loaf using the same recipe but simply use 600g wholemeal bread flour instead of the oatmeal, soya and wholemeal flours.

Boiled Raisin Cake

Makes about 12 slices

200g raisins
250ml water
100ml groundnut oil
150ml cold water
200g light soft brown sugar
300g flour (see Tip)
2 level tsps mixed spice
1 heaped tsp baking powder
1 tsp salt

Boil the raisins in the first lot of water for 15 minutes in a saucepan, then remove from the heat and add the groundnut oil and cold water.

Mix together the sugar, flour, spice, baking powder and salt in a large bowl, then add the raisin mixture and stir till combined.

Pour into a lightly oiled 20cm-round cake tin lined with parchment. Pre-heat the oven to 170°C and bake for an hour. Check after the hour – it is done when a skewer comes out clean from the centre. If not cooked, put it back in the oven for another 10 minutes and check again. Leave to go completely cold in the tin.

TIP

You can use standard white flour or a mix of white and wholemeal.

Almond Butter Biscuits

Makes about 18 smallish biscuits
Fresh ingredient: butter

125g ground almonds
100g wholewheat flour
75g plain white flour
level tsp salt
level tsp ground cinnamon
100ml runny honey
120g butter

Put the ground almonds, flours, salt and cinnamon into a mixing bowl and combine thoroughly.

Heat the honey and butter in a saucepan until the butter is just melted, then leave to cool until barely warm (see Tip), stir and pour into the dry mix. Using a fork, combine well, adding a little cold water if the mix doesn't come together as a fairly dry dough.

Break off pieces about the size of a dessertspoon bowl and form gently into balls. Place them on a non-stick baking tray and press each down to flatten to about 1cm thick, leaving at least 4cm space in between each.

Bake in the oven at 170°C for about 30 minutes, until the edges begin to turn brown. Transfer to wire racks to cool, then store in an airtight container.

TIP

If you add the honey and butter mix to the flours while it is still hot, it will encourage the ground almonds to release their oils and this might toughen the biscuits.

Pineapple Oatmeal Cookies

Makes about 20–24 large cookies

250g oatmeal
250g wholewheat flour
75g shredded coconut
125g chopped walnuts
125g raisins
2 tsps baking powder
1 tsp salt
400g can pineapple chunks in juice
pineapple or apple juice (about 100ml)
4 tbsps water
2 tsps vanilla extract
175ml runny honey

In large bowl, combine the first seven (dry) ingredients. Drain the pineapple from its juice, so that the juice runs into a measuring bowl or jug. Add enough pineapple or apple juice to this to make up 225ml in total. Divide the pineapple pieces in half.

Now using a hand blender, mix the water, vanilla extract, honey and half the pineapple, then add the juice and combine well. Mix the contents of the dry bowl with the wet bowl, add the reserved pineapple pieces and stir in well.

Drop tablespoons of the mixture on to a lightly oiled non-stick baking sheet and cook in the oven at 170°C for 12 minutes or until golden. Allow to cool a little, then finish cooling on a wire rack before storing in an airtight tin.

The cookies will keep for a day or two.

Chocolate and Peanut Butter Cookies

Makes 10

150ml maple or golden syrup
60ml groundnut oil
25g cocoa powder
level tsp ground cinnamon
100g crunchy peanut butter
150g rolled oats
1 tsp vanilla extract

Put the maple syrup, oil, cocoa powder and cinnamon in a non-stick saucepan over a medium-low heat. Bring to a simmer and, stirring constantly, simmer for 2–3 minutes.

Remove the pan from the heat and stir in the peanut butter, rolled oats and vanilla until well blended.

Drop dessertspoonfuls of the mixture on to a non-stick baking tray, and chill for about 30 minutes until set. Transfer to an airtight container to store.

American Pear Cake

Makes about 12 slices

Fresh ingredients: eggs, apple purée, pears (optional)

100ml apple purée (see Tip)
75ml extra-virgin groundnut or rapeseed oil
160g soft light brown sugar
2 eggs, beaten
1 tsp vanilla extract
125g plain white flour
125g wholewheat flour
2 tsps baking powder
½ tsp salt
1 tsp mixed spice
3 medium dessert pears, peeled, cored and chopped
    (see Tip)
100g chopped pecan nuts or almonds

Lightly brush a 1kg cake tin or bundt tin (see Tip) with groundnut oil. In a mixing bowl, whisk together the apple purée, oil and brown sugar, blending thoroughly. Add the egg a tablespoonful at a time, whisking well after each addition, then add the vanilla.

Put the flours, baking powder, salt and spice into another mixing bowl and gradually add the wet mixture, stirring thoroughly, then stir in the pears and nuts.

Spoon the batter into the prepared tin and bake the cake for an hour at 170°C, or until a skewer put into the centre of the cake comes out clean. Cool in the tin for 10 minutes before turning out on to a wire rack to continue cooling. Store in an airtight tin.

TIPS

This American pear cake-cum-dessert is usually cooked in a bundt tin – a circular baking tin with a hole in the centre – but you can use any shape of cake tin you have to hand. A traditional cake tin may increase the cooking time a little.

You can use home-bottled pears in this recipe (see pages 195–6), or a jar or can of bought pear halves – one 500g can or jar, drained, will contain around six pear halves.

You can use ready-made apple purée (baby purée is fine, and so is apple sauce), or, to make your own, peel one large or two smaller cooking apples (preferably Bramleys) and chop the flesh into a saucepan with 1 tbsp water and 1 tbsp sugar. Bring to a simmer and cook over a medium heat, stirring occasionally, until the apples purée up – this will take only about 10 minutes. If your cooking apples are not the sort, like Bramleys, that do pulp up very easily, then help them along by mashing with a potato masher. If necessary, you can use a hand blender on low afterwards to finish the puréeing process, but cool the apple mixture first.

If you make surplus apple purée, or make it when you have a glut, you can freeze it or bottle it in sterilized jars, which you should then sterilize as explained on page 189.

11 Festive Occasions and Gifts

Once you've got the hang of making your own preserves, chutneys, flavoured oils and so on, you will have lifelong inspiration for what to give people for presents, as well as a range of goodies you can make yourself to brighten your own table on festive occasions.

If you hate roaming round the shops looking for presents and getting home laden (but with a much lighter purse), then you will save all that bother, and some expense too.

This chapter contains a few ideas for such special occasions. I've even added a couple of easy chocolate recipes, which you should try. Put into pretty boxes or baskets, they are sure to make you no. 1 favourite person in the recipient's eyes, at least for a while!

Of course any of the preserves or pickles in previous chapters will also provide welcome gifts.

Flavoured oils

Home-made flavoured oils make a superb gift and are not difficult to do. All you need are some sterilized, suitably decorative bottles or jars, good oils (not just olive oil but also sesame oil and groundnut oil, for example) and your choice of spices and/or herbs. Below are some simple recipes for mixes which will be appreciated by friends and will also be a great addition to your own larder. All are excellent for use in cooking and can also be used in salads or sauces, while most are good as a dip for bread.

First a few general tips:

- Herbs grown outdoors and harvested in midsummer will be more robust and stronger tasting than those force-grown in the winter or harvested in spring.

- Herbs are best picked just before they flower.

- Herbs should be perfectly dry before adding to the oil – by that I don't mean you have to use actual dried herbs, but that any fresh herbs should be clean and bone dry. If you have your own herbs, pick them when the sun has been on them for a few hours, if possible. Don't pick in early morning, as they may be dew covered. The aroma and flavour also improves after a few hours in the sun.

- Whole spices should be dry too.

- You can add ground spices, but they can 'cloud' the oil – whole or cracked are a better idea.

- Garlic can be added, but as even 'old' garlic contains quite a high level of moisture it may not last as long as other flavoured oils. For your own use, you can remove the garlic cloves from the oil after a few weeks, if you like.

- Buy the best-quality oils that you can – the end result is largely dependent upon this. For more information on choosing oils, see Chapter 2, page 68–73, and the A–Z.

- Marry the flavourings you choose to a suitable oil – some examples are given below.

- Only use perfectly clean, dry, pre-sterilized containers – see page 170.

- In all the recipes below, after making your oil, put a sterilized lid or cork on your container and store in a dry place.

- Steeping period: after making, flavoured oils are best kept for a week or so, so that the herbs or spices have time to flavour the oil.

- Once opened, flavoured oils should be used up within a couple of weeks. Some chefs recommend straining the oils after a few weeks of marinading to remove the herbs or spices, but I don't think this is strictly necessary in most cases.

- Beware food poisoning! Fresh garlic and other spices and herbs can be a potential source of food poisoning. For this reason, if children, the elderly or the sick will be using oils containing these things, it is wise to remove them after the steeping period.

- You can also be doubly safe by heating the oil with chilli and/or garlic to 180°C in a pan before pouring it into the containers. This method helps

the flavours to release and also helps kill any bacteria which may be present – but the taste of the oil will suffer slightly. Don't heat oil when making green-leaf-flavoured oils.

- As most herbs and spices are very rich sources of antioxidants and most have antibacterial properties of their own, I personally think that you would be unlikely to suffer any problems with these flavoured oils even if you don't pre-heat or strain, as long as you follow the other tips, use sterilized containers and don't keep the oils for too long.

- You can buy labels and write your own description – for gifts it is a good idea to list exactly what is in the bottle, and, if you can be bothered, you might also write a little card suggesting uses.

- If you're going to use any of the herb-containing oils for high-temperature cooking, such as frying, the amount of oil you need should be filtered through a fine sieve to remove any herbs, which could burn. Obviously if you filter the oils after the steeping period, this won't be necessary.

- For where to buy suitable containers, see Larder accessories in the A–Z (page 239).

All the amounts of flavourings suggested are based on your filling 2 x 500ml bottles or jars (or, obviously, a single 1-litre container) with your chosen oil. For more detailed instructions on the bottling process, see the general tips on page 215.

Provençal-flavoured Oil

Put a few whole sprigs of rosemary, a small handful of oregano leaves, 2 small bay leaves and a handful of thyme sprigs in each container and then fill with French or Italian extra-virgin olive oil. If you like you can include one or two French lavender flowers.

Basil Oil

Follow the recipe on page 193 for basil preserved in oil (preferably Italian first-pressing olive oil), but use less basil and more oil. For a lovely oil to use as a base for basil pesto, or a tomato salad dressing or dip for crusty Italian bread, add 4–6 peeled cloves of garlic (depending on size) as well.

Chilli Oil

Add 4–8 dried red chillies (depending on size) – and 4–6 peeled cloves of garlic to sesame oil or, if you prefer a lighter taste, one-third sesame oil and two-thirds groundnut oil. Excellent for Thai dishes.

See note on page 215–6 about pre-heating chilli and garlic oil before bottling.

For information on drying your own whole chillies, see page 199.

Ginger and Garlic Oil

Peel 75g fresh root ginger and cut into 1cm cubes, then lightly bruise it (using a rolling pin or clean meat cleaver to bash it), add 2–4 peeled garlic cloves and put into sterilized containers filled with groundnut oil. Good for chicken and pork oriental dishes.

Garlic Oil

Omit the ginger in the previous recipe and use more garlic (up to 10 cloves depending on how strong you want it). Good in many Chinese recipes.

See note opposite about pre-heating fresh spice oil before bottling.

Mint Oil

Pick 2–3 good handfuls of fresh mint leaves (peppermint or apple mint are my favourites) – you can leave smallish stalks on if you like – and add them to a fairly light olive oil. This is good drizzled over lamb before roasting, used as an oil to sauté chicken and baby broad beans in summer, or drizzled over new potatoes.

Mixed Spice Oil

Add 1 level tbsp each of whole coriander seeds, allspice and black peppercorns, plus 1 tsp of juniper berries to groundnut or light olive oil. Good, filtered, for pre-frying onions for Indian dishes.

Pepper Oil

Put 1 tbsp each of red, white and black whole peppercorns in a mortar and crush very lightly with the pestle, then add to your containers with a robust olive oil, such as Greek, or a mix of half sesame and half groundnut or sunflower oil. If you prefer, the corns can be added whole.

Flavoured Vinegars

Like flavoured oils, vinegars are another simple gift to make at home. The secret lies in choosing good-quality vinegars and selecting the right ones to complement the chosen flavours.

One of the beauties of vinegar is that it is a natural preservative and so the flavoured vinegars should last a long time – but they need to be stored in the dark, as light affects the colour, especially of paler vinegars. You still need to pre-sterilize the containers and make sure they are completely dry when you use them (see page 170). The colour of the herbs will also alter – fade and darken – with time and so the vinegars are always best strained once the steeping period is over.

Below are a few of my favourite flavoured vinegars with some suggestions for use. You can more or less invent your own mixes, as you like.

All the amounts of flavourings suggested are based on you filling 2 x 500ml bottles or jars (or, obviously, a single 1-litre container) with vinegar. Read the general tips listed for flavoured oils on pages 215–6, most of which will also apply to flavoured vinegars.

Tarragon Vinegar

Use French tarragon rather than Russian, as the flavour is much finer. A pot of French tarragon will grow happily on a warm terrace or in a sunny corner of the garden, but should be treated as an annual in most UK gardens as it isn't that hardy.

Pick the tarragon and strip away the larger woody stalks carefully, leaving the elongated leaves and just a few of the non-woody stalks. Use 2 handfuls of tarragon in each 500ml container.

Fill the sterilized jars with white wine vinegar or cider vinegar, put sterilized lids on and leave in a dark, dry place for 2–4 weeks.

Now strain the vinegar (through muslin or a very fine sieve) and remove the leaves before replacing the strained vinegar in a new sterilized container (see page 170). For a gift, you can pop a whole stalk of tarragon in, if you have one.

Tarragon vinegar can be used instead of plain vinegar in a salad dressing for cold cooked chicken.

Mint Vinegar

Pick a large bunch of fresh mint, remove the stalks and roughly chop the leaves before putting them in your sterilized containers. Pour over white wine vinegar or a good-quality light malt vinegar to fill the containers completely and cover the mint, and put the sterilized lids on. Store for 4–6 weeks, then strain and bottle the vinegar in a new sterilized container (see page 170).

Mint vinegar can be used with olive oil to make a dressing for a potato or bean salad, or with oil as a marinade for lamb.

Chilli Vinegar

Good for using up a glut of chillies. Halve as many fresh red or green chillies as you like (I would suggest about 20) and add them to white wine vinegar in a pan. Bring to the boil, remove from the heat and decant into your prepared sterilized bottles (see page 170). Leave for a few weeks then strain and re-bottle as above.

I found one recipe that suggested 60 chillies – but that is up to you!

Marinated Goat's Cheese

Makes 2 x 250ml jars

Fresh ingredient: goat's cheese

600ml extra-virgin olive oil (see Tip)
1 heaped tbsp thyme leaves
1 heaped tbsp mixed peppercorns
1 level dsp dried red chilli flakes
4 cloves garlic, peeled
400g log of goat's cheese

Pour the olive oil into two wide-necked sterilized jars until each is a third full. Divide the thyme, peppercorns and chilli between the two jars. Finely chop the garlic and put that in, then slice the cheese and divide that between the jars. Top up with olive oil until the cheese is completely covered, put sterilized lids on securely, and gently shake each jar to distribute the flavourings. Leave to marinate in a cold, dry place for two weeks, shaking the jars once every couple of days.

Once opened, eat within a couple of days.

TIP

A fruity, green olive oil is good in this recipe. See Chapter 2, page 71, and the A–Z for suggestions.

Olives with Preserved Lemons

Makes 2 x 250g jars

250g large, stoned green olives
1 preserved lemon, drained and chopped (see Tip)
1 level dsp oregano leaves
250ml extra-virgin olive oil

Drain the olives as necessary (see Tip) and divide them into your sterilized jars with the lemon and oregano, then top up each jar to the brim with olive oil. Put the sterilized lids on, shake to combine, and store for 2 weeks before using.

Once opened, use within 1–2 weeks and store in the fridge.

TIPS

You can buy jars of preserved lemons in all good food stores.

The large green olives you can buy loose in the deli will be fine in this recipe.

The finished olives are perfect to accompany an aperitif such as dry sherry.

Spiced Olives

Makes 2 x 250g jars

250g stoned black olives from a jar (see Tip)
1 tsp dried red chilli flakes
1 tsp whole allspice
2 large cloves garlic, peeled and chopped
1 tsp brown mustard seeds
1 dsp thyme leaves
250ml extra-virgin olive oil

Drain the olives thoroughly, then put them in your sterilized jars with all the seasonings. Pour over the oil and shake, then put sterilized lids on and store for 2 weeks before using.

The olives should keep unopened in a cool place for a few weeks. Once opened, use within a week or so and keep in the fridge.

TIPS

Use ordinary black olives or try the kalamata variety, which has a superior taste.

These olives are great chopped into a spicy leaf salad, using a little of the oil from the jar in the dressing. They are also great as an appetizer before dinner.

Christmas Chutney

Makes 3–4 x 400g jars

Fresh ingredient: onions

400g onions, peeled and finely chopped
350g stoned ready-to-eat prunes, finely chopped
275g stoned semi-dried dates, finely chopped
275g ready-to-eat dried apricots, finely chopped
2 cloves garlic, peeled and chopped
500ml red wine vinegar
400g dark soft brown sugar
2 tbsps sea salt flakes
1 heaped tsp ground ginger
2 tbsps allspice berries
3cm piece cinnamon

Put the onions in a large, lidded pan with 75ml water, bring to a simmer and cook for 10 minutes until softened, then add all the dried fruits and the garlic and simmer for another 5 minutes.

Now pour the vinegar into the pan and add the sugar, salt and ginger. Put the allspice and cinnamon in a muslin bag and add to the pan. Over a low heat, without the lid on, dissolve the sugar, stirring frequently.

Leave to cook very gently without a lid for about 1½ hours, or until the chutney has thickened, stirring from time to time.

When it's ready, you will be able to draw a spoon across the base of the pan and make a trail in the chutney that takes a second or two to disappear.

Have sterilized warm jars ready (see page 170). Remove the muslin bag, spoon the mixture into the warmed jars, cover with waxed discs and tight sterilized lids, and store in a cool, dark, dry place.

TIPS

This dark, spicy chutney is delicious with cold turkey, ham or goose, pork pies or any strong cheese. Leave the made chutney for about a month to mature in the jars before eating.

Once opened, store in the fridge and eat within a couple of weeks.

Mincemeat

Makes 2 x 400g jars
Fresh ingredients: lemon, cooking apple, butter

250g mixed dried fruit
100g dried dates, finely chopped
75g glacé cherries, chopped
50ml brandy
juice of 1 lemon
200g cooking apple
1 tbsp butter
60g soft dark brown sugar
1 tbsp golden syrup
50g chopped mixed nuts
1 tsp mixed spice
½ tsp each ground cloves and nutmeg

Put the mixed fruit, dates and cherries in a mixing bowl. Combine the brandy and lemon juice and pour over the fruit. Cover and leave overnight.

When you're ready to make the mincemeat, peel, core and roughly chop the apple. Heat the butter gently in a large, non-stick pan and fry the apple until it is soft (see Tip)– it doesn't want colour on it.

Now tip all the fruit from the mixing bowl into the frying pan, stir in all the other ingredients and combine well. Cook gently for 20 minutes, stirring a few times.

Spoon the hot mix into warm sterilized jars (see page 170) and put sterilized lids on.

The mincemeat will keep for several weeks in a cool, dry place.

TIPS

If you use Bramleys they will disintegrate; other cooking apples may stay in their whole pieces. Either is OK – but I prefer Bramleys.

You can add 100g of shredded suet to the mix if you want to be more traditional – either vegetarian or non-vegetarian, that is up to you; both are fine.

Use the mincemeat to make mince pies at Christmas, or add to apples or pears in a fruit tart or crumble. You can also heat it and serve over ice cream.

Brandy Truffles

Makes about 24

Fresh ingredients: butter, double cream

200g dark chocolate
60g butter at room temperature
50ml double cream
3 heaped tbsps icing sugar
20ml brandy
cocoa powder for dusting

Break the chocolate into small pieces and put in a heatproof bowl which will fit snugly over a saucepan in which you can simmer a few centimetres of water without the base of the bowl touching the water.

Add the butter to the bowl and melt the chocolate butter mix over barely simmering water, then stir in the cream, remove from the heat and allow to cool until just warm. Stir in the icing sugar and then the brandy.

Leave in the fridge or a cool place, covered, for several hours. When it is cold, make little balls (gently, using clean, cool hands) and place them on a baking tray, then dredge thoroughly with cocoa powder.

> **TIP**
>
> Put 12 truffles into each of two cellophane bags and tie with pretty ribbon for two good Christmas gifts.

Treacle Toffee

Makes about 3 x 250g bags

Fresh ingredient: butter

500g black treacle
500g brown cane sugar
30g butter
1 tsp vanilla extract

Put the treacle into a non-stick saucepan with the sugar and butter over a low heat and cook until melted, stirring frequently.

Turn up the heat and bring to the boil, stirring. Turn down the heat so that the mixture has a strong simmer and cook for 15 minutes, stirring from time to time.

To test whether the toffee is ready, drop a teaspoonful into cold water. If it solidifies, it is ready.

Add the vanilla, pour into a lightly oiled, non-stick, shallow tin and mark into small squares with a sharp knife before it gets completely cold. When cold, break into pieces and put in cellophane bags tied with ribbon.

> **TIP**
>
> For nut toffee, add chopped nuts to the simmering mix.

Berry Fruit Coulis

Makes about 3 x 250ml bottles
Fresh ingredients: berries, lemon

1.25kg fresh (or frozen) berries of choice (see Tip),
   de-stalked and washed as necessary
approx. 150g icing sugar
juice of 1 lemon

Put the fruit in an electric blender if you have one
with 3 tbsps water and blend to a purée. If you
don't have a blender, mash the fruit thoroughly in
a large bowl with a fork.

Press through a sieve into a saucepan and stir in
the icing sugar and lemon juice. Bring to a simmer
over a medium heat and cook for a minute, no
more, then decant into sterilized bottles, put
in sterilized corks (boiled for 10 minutes then
thoroughly dried) and store in a cool, dark,
dry place.

This will keep for a few weeks.

TIPS

Coulis is always a welcome gift for birthdays or thank
yous, as it is quite expensive to buy and often far too
sweet.

You can make a good coulis with many different fruits,
but my favourites are brightly coloured berry coulis. My
number one is an equal mix of blackcurrants, redcurrants
and raspberries, but I have also used blackcurrants,
raspberries and strawberries. You could replace the
blackcurrants with blueberries, or the raspberries
with loganberries. I add lemon juice because I think it
improves the flavour, but if you don't have a lemon it
isn't the end of the world – a tablespoon of balsamic
vinegar would achieve a similar effect.

You can use frozen berries – most supermarkets sell
bags of frozen mixed berries.

The amount of sugar you need to produce the right level
of sharp sweetness will depend upon the proportions of
fruit and type of fruits used. Blackcurrants are extremely
sharp, so if you use a lot of them you may need to increase
the amount of sugar – taste at heating stage and add
extra sugar if you need to.

Berry coulis is an ideal accompaniment to sponge and
chocolate cakes, ice cream, drizzled over breakfast
yogurt, with pancakes or with chocolate desserts.

Mulled Red Wine

Makes 1.5 litres
Fresh ingredient: orange

1 litre good robust red wine (e.g. Shiraz)
500ml red grape juice
zest of 1 orange, cut into strips
1 large cinnamon stick
6 cloves
2 tsps crushed cardamom pods
1 tsp grated nutmeg
100ml brandy

Put all the ingredients except the brandy into a
large saucepan or preserving pan and bring to the
boil, then take off the heat, stir in the brandy and
serve in heatproof glasses with handles.

TIPS

If you don't want your spices and peel floating about in
the wine, put everything into a muslin bag.

You might like to add a couple of tablespoons of caster sugar to the wine if you prefer a sweeter taste – this would need to be added as the wine comes to the boil, so that it dissolves, and you would need to stir the pan a few times to ensure this. You can also add the juice from the orange to the mix, if you like.

You can use a similar recipe for mulled cider – choose 1 litre medium-dry cider, ½ litre good-quality apple juice and you can if you like use local cider brandy or calvados instead of brandy. Or you can omit the brandy altogether for a milder mull.

Eliza Acton's Cherry Brandy

Makes 2 x 1 litre bottles
Fresh ingredients: Morello cherries

1kg just-ripe Morello cherries
200g sugar
brandy to cover (see Tip)

Destalk the cherries (though this isn't strictly necessary) and divide between two wide-necked sterilized bottles (see page 170), then divide the sugar between them.

Pour in brandy to fill the bottles up to the neck, put on the sterilized lids or corks and stand for up to 2 months before using.

TIPS

You can decant the brandy to drink, and eat the cherries. Mrs Beeton has a similar recipe and says that the bottles of unopened cherry brandy will last for years.

Morello cherries should be in the shops in late summer.

PART 3 Resources

12 A–Z OF INGREDIENTS

In this resources section I have gathered together information on brands, where to buy and other tips on stocking your storecupboard with foods you will really want to eat and ingredients with which you will really want to cook.

Ingredients are listed alphabetically so everything is easy to find. In general, I have grouped like things together: for example, if you want to find almonds, you will need to look up 'Nuts'.

Biscuits

Plain digestives (McVitie's are still the best) are useful crushed as bases for cheesecake or added to crumble toppings. A packet of biscotti – hard, crunchy, not-too-sweet Italian biscuits – is a good standby for coffee with friends. Try almond or chocolate and hazelnut – from www.terreaterre.co.uk or Carluccio's biscotti Toscani assortiti (www.carluccios.com). Or try real American imported cookies (various) from www.americansweets.co.uk, or Fudges' Chocolate Florentines (a halfway house between a biscuit and a chocolate – www.fudges.co.uk).

Breads and bread products

When the bread bin is empty there are several useful longlife bread-type items you can find in a well-stocked larder. I always keep a packet of wraps – large, soft, wheat – from any supermarket (Mission Deli Wraps are a favourite) to fill as a change from ordinary sandwiches. Or try Fudges' (www.fudges.co.uk) sesame and pumpkin or spelt flatbreads – smaller and great with dips. Tortillas are similar to wraps but may be made of corn or wheat and may be thicker.

A packet of longlife pittas is useful (e.g. Newbury Phillips organic white or wholemeal pittas) to split and fill with salad, chicken, tuna, chickpeas, etc., while tacos are an alternative. And for a family, a packet of organic mini pizza bases (Biona brand, from www.pulseorganics.com), would be handy for a quick supper.

Packets of ready-sliced dark rye bread usually have a long shelf-life and can be used for open sandwiches or cut into four for canapé bases (Mestemacher German Bread Basket, www.goodnessdirect.co.uk). Or for something rather different and very healthy, try Sunnyvale Organic Sprouted Hemp Bread or, interestingly, Biona Organic Corn and Lupin Bread (both www.goodnessdirect.co.uk) which will last for months until you open the packet.

You can buy packets of longlife ready-made crostini – crusty, hard-baked Italian bread slices ideal for topping with tapenade or avocado and tomato (www.carluccios.com) – or melba or French toasts. You may also like some good-quality grissini (breadsticks – cheap ones are usually not nice, but try Organico Classic Grissini – www.pulseorganics.com). Lastly, if you can wait an hour or so, you could whip up a home-made loaf with a quick bread mix (e.g. Wright's multigrain, widely available) which contains its own yeast and needs only one rising. Much nicer than those longlife part-baked sticks you can buy.

Breakfast cereals

You probably don't need me to tell you much about breakfast cereals, as they are some of the most familiar items in the shopping trolley. But I urge you to stock up with healthier varieties, rather than the highly refined and/or sweetened types. A well-made muesli is one of the best starts to the day – try the Dorset Cereals range (widely available). I have also found a great low-cost muesli at Aldi called Harvest Morn. You don't necessarily want the one with the most fruit in it – 45 per cent nuts and fruit is plenty. You want one with plenty of oats: check the ingredients label, as lots of mueslis contain more wheat flakes than oats or rye, both of which are in my opinion better flakes for breakfast as they keep you feeling satisfied for longer than wheat. Apricot muesli from www.countryproducts.co.uk is a wonderful example and a good price as well.

Porridge is, of course, a good winter start – go for traditional rolled oats (e.g. Jordans Organic Porridge Oats (widely available), or Pertwood Organic Porridge Oats – from the Co-op or www.ethicalsuperstore.com.

Cakes and desserts

For the larder, you want a cake that will keep and that isn't too delicate. Fruit cakes are ideal as they often improve with keeping. Then, of course, you want a cake that tastes as if it is home-made, as you will, naturally, be using the cake only when someone you want to impress arrives at coffee or tea time. Thus my recommendations aren't cheap. Try Meg Rivers' almond fruit cake (www.megrivers.com) or a baked-in-a-box fruit cake from www.incrediblefruitcake.com. Fudges' (www.fudges.com) seasonal cakes for Christmas include a lovely stollen and panetonne, which keep for several weeks, and are widely available in shops before the festive season.

Other cake or dessert-ish everyday ideas for the larder include flapjacks (great for lunchboxes – try Fudges); Biona organic apple and pear waffles (www.goodnessdirect.co.uk), nice with maple syrup and ice cream. And, of course, trifle sponges are a must, and brandy-snap baskets are a lovely instant pudding if you have any cream in the fridge, with some Morello or black cherries (out of a jar, if you like). A jar of Carluccio's Zabajone con Moscato (a kind of zabaglione in a jar) is worth keeping – once opened it will all be gone, though . . .

You might also stock some dulce de leche – the soft caramel that is used in banoffee pie and for other desserts. Merchant Gourmet dulce de leche or Nestlé's Carnation Caramel are both stocked at Waitrose.

Store all cakes in an airtight tin.

Chocolate and confectionery

If you don't have a fresh pudding and feel like something sweet at the end of a meal, a morsel (or more!) of some tasty sweetmeat or other that you can produce from your stores will fill the gap well. Try authentic Gulluoglu Turkish Delight (e.g. double pistachio), imported by www.turkiyeden.com

Or try turron, which is like a top-range halva nougat, an almonds-and-honey-rich treat from Spain – delicious! Try the Organic Collection Jijona (soft) Turron (www.graigfarm.co.uk or www.goodnessdirect.co.uk). Marzipan lovers will go for Graig Farm's superb, top-quality, dark-chocolate-enrobed marzipan from Germany – slice it thinly and eat with raspberries or raspberry coulis (Best of Taste, from www.realfooddirect.co.uk).

We all cook with chocolate sometimes – I use ordinary eating chocolate with around 70 per cent cocoa solids which I think gives a better flavour than 'cooking chocolate'. If you want a low-cost one, try Lidl's dark chocolate, or the Co-op's fairtrade dark chocolate. If you're keeping chocolate in the larder, hidden from the kids, to eat as it is – try the Chocolate Society's Valrhona Carre de Caraibe Grand Cru – 18 squares in a metal tin, handy for the larder, or, perhaps more sensibly, try their cooking chocolate pieces (www.chocolate.co.uk or Waitrose).

Chocolate spread is a great treat for toast or oatcakes – I like Green & Black's Hazelnut Chocolate Spread (widely available). And you also need some proper drinking chocolate (www.chocolate.co.uk).

Chutneys, pickles and relishes

Even if you make your own chutney it's handy to have one or two jars of ready-made chutney available – and you can find some real specialities these days. The local Country Market (previously WI markets) will have a good range, especially if you're looking for local, in-season chutneys. Find out where your nearest market is at www.country-markets.co.uk.

Ethnic food shops are another great source, especially for hot, spicy and unusual chutneys. www.spicewarehouse.com has good pickles. But I have found one or two good mass-market brands – Patak's Brinjal Pickle is made from aubergines and is good with cold meats or cheese, not just your curry. Most

lime pickle is too hot for me, but my husband says that his favourite is Hot Lime Pickle (www.redhotchillipeople.com).

For less mainstream chutneys (e.g. carrot chutney or chilli jelly), try www.finerpreserves.co.uk (01377 249430), a smallish Yorkshire company who have won awards, or visit www.kitchengardenpreserves.co.uk, whose organic hand-made chutneys have also won awards. Or try www.tracklements.co.uk or www.dukeshillham.co.uk.

www.terreaterre.co.uk do a wonderful soft onion merlot marmalade, great with cheese and in sandwiches. Visit www.delicioso.co.uk, the good Spanish food store who stock authentic Spanish membrillo (quince jelly) to serve with manchego cheese.

Cooking marinades, pastes and ingredients

There are so many hundreds in this important, flavour-enhancing category to choose from, in each ethnic area, that it is almost impossible for me to narrow the selection down to a few – apart from which, people's tastes vary.

My own essentials include sauces or pastes I would never consider making myself – soya sauce, yellow and black bean sauce, for example, or hoisin, mustard, ketjap manis, fish sauce, tahini (sesame seed paste), one or two chilli sauces, and shrimp paste, for a start. And when buying these, my advice is simple: go for the best quality you can (which is often but not always reflected in the price). You use so little to make a meal that it is a false economy to try to save money.

Things that are quick and easy to make yourself – such as tapenade, or a pesto, or simple Thai green curry paste, aren't such storecupboard essentials, but if you can find a good brand you may still prefer to stock than make. Carluccio's online store (www.carluccios.com), or stores throughout the UK, have fabulous Italian ingredients, including pesto Genovese, and pomodorata, sundried tomato and caper paste. Oil & Vinegar shops (for stores see www.oilvinegar.com, no online sales) have a lovely Romesco paste with tomatoes, nuts, oil and vinegar.

Try www.theasiancookshop.co.uk or www.tigertiger.info for a good selection of Indian, Chinese and Thai ingredients, or try www.ethicalsuperstore.com for whole world foods. Tesco www.tesco.com and the other supermarkets carry a good range of chilli sauces, such as Lingham's ginger, garlic and chilli sauce and the new, very very hot Tabasco Habanero sauce. www.wallysdeli.co.uk has fabulous things, from minced lemon grass to Bevelini Italian pestos. www.pulseorganics.com has a large selection of organic pastes and ingredients, including organic Sacla tomato pesto and organic Worcester sauce.

For marinades and dry rubs, try NoMu Rubs from www.barbecue-online.co.uk and at the same site you will also find a good teriyaki marinade – Soy Vay veri veri.

Good harissa can be found at www.belazu.com – it is Belazu Rose Harissa, good for marinades but also great in many other dishes. www.maroque.co.uk has *harissa traditionelle*.

Cooking sauces

I would tend to ignore all those packets of dried sauce mixes, however tempting the idea – often they are under-flavoured, strange-textured, and/or over-salted. If you want a ready-made sauce, such as a tomato and basil sauce for pasta, or a red wine sauce for a casserole, and really don't have the energy to make your own (nearly as quick!), then you can find some decent brands, again, at www.ethicalsuperstore.com. In my experience, organically produced sauces tend to be tastier and to have fewer E numbers than non-organic, and sauces in jars seem to be better than those in cans or pouches (but that's only my opinion). For spice lovers, www.theasiancookshop.co.uk has various cooking sauces. Meridian cooking sauces are great and tasty, and are suitable for people who want to avoid items such as wheat, gluten or dairy. For pasta sauces, Carluccio's comes into its own, with a big range including clam sauce (vongole), walnut sauce (salsa di noci), mushroom and truffle, and wild fennel (www.carluccios.com). Pasta sauces from Kitchen Garden are also good (from www.ethicalsuperstore.com).

Crispbreads and crackers

You need a cheese-biscuit selection (try Fudges – www.fudges.co.uk) or some good oatcakes (try Ditty's Irish oatcakes or Duchy Originals Oaten Biscuits) and some water biscuits (nothing wrong with Carrs), and Bath Olivers or Oval Alberts (from www.dukeshillham. co.uk). If you are watching your weight, get some wholegrain rice cakes (Kallo are fine) and some thin wholegrain crispbreads – Ryvita multigrain or dark rye are good quality, but Dr Karg Classic 3-Seed are even better. Rakusen's 99% Crackers are only 18 calories each. For people watching their salt intake, try Rakusen's fat-free wheaten matzos with no added salt or fat.

Try for a treat Fudges Jalapeno or Walnut Wafers or, for Marmite addicts, their now-famous Marmite biscuits (www.fudges.co.uk). Waitrose have a really good selection of savoury biscuits: www.waitrosedeliver.com.

A packet of quick-cook poppadoms may be handy: www.spicesofindia.co.uk have a great range, including some made from rice.

Dairy products and eggs

When you are talking dairy for the larder, then the items are going to be 'stand-bys' rather than your first choice, which, if you are sensible, will be fresh. That said, over the years I often found myself using longlife skimmed milk in Tetra Paks (a large household, a remote home and being very busy often meant we unintentionally ran out of the real thing). The skimmed version is quite OK in coffee, recipes and so on. My kids used to have a thing for longlife custard – either canned or in Tetra Paks. Ambrosia was their favourite. I've even served it, with a little vanilla extract added, in trifles for grown-ups and they were quite edible.

A good longlife cream that can be stored ambient is hard to come by, in my experience, but a can of Nestlé's Carnation condensed milk might do the trick if you have a very sweet tooth. (This can also be boiled for 3 hours to make dulce de leche – see *Cakes and desserts*, page 232.) Packets of dessert topping mix, to which you add milk and which are supposed to taste like cream, are stuffed full of hydrogenated (unhealthy) fats, so don't get those for the kids.

A couple of jars of feta or goat's cheese in oil are a good standby for salads, recipes and sandwiches. You can often find chunks of feta combined with items such as black olives, red peppers or herbs, which may make a change. And there are Lorea Gourmet rolled anchovies with manchego cheese preserved in olive oil (Waitrose). In a cool larder you can also store Stilton in a jar – Cropwell Bishop is one of the best – buy from Fortnum & Mason, or try www. paxtonandwhitfield.co.uk.

Lastly, if you have a cool larder you can store very fresh eggs for short periods without refrigeration (but to be on the safe side I would not serve them to the sick, young or elderly, and would cook them well, unless stamped with the Lion, certifying that the hens were salmonella-vaccinated).

You may also like to have a packet of Supercook pasteurized whole-egg powder (www.supercookonline.co.uk) – one packet replaces 10 eggs.

If you want to store something different for your dairy fix, try Borden's Egg Nog (www.americansweets.co.uk) – a mix of egg yolks, cream and milk. It will keep for months unopened and, chilled, makes a good, if calorific, drink.

Flour and pastry

Flour of all kinds is best bought in fairly small amounts and used within a few weeks. Store it in airtight, bug-proof containers and keep away from damp. Good basic wheat flours for baking and bread-making can be found in all the supermarkets. A basic range might be plain white (all-purpose) flour, wholewheat flour, strong plain flour. Graig Farm (www.grainfarm.co.uk) have a selection of quality organic Doves and Bacheldre flours, including spelt flour and durum wheat pasta flour. People with allergies to wheat will find a good selection of other types of flour at www.goodnessdirect.co.uk. You may find it useful to keep a small packet of arrowroot – a flour which goes transparent on heating with liquid and is ideal for desserts and sauces. Sauce flour (e.g. Carrs Sauce Flour, from supermarkets) is another option – very fine and easy to make into good savoury béchamels, etc. For people on a diet it is good because it will thicken a sauce without need for fat.

For fast canapés I can recommend Rahms mini croustades – delicately thin and crisp-baked pastry shells to fill yourself. Fudges cheese straws are another good standby for nibbles with drinks (www.fudges.co.uk). I haven't found really excellent larder-store ready-baked pastry shells for quiches, tarts and so on (although Tesco's Finest All-Butter Pastry Case isn't too bad). A speedy compromise might be to make your own using a pastry mix (find these with the flours in the supermarket).

Fish

You don't need me to tell you about canned tuna, and red and pink salmon. But these days the producers are trying hard to tempt us with more variety on the canned fish shelves. For example, you can find sardines in oil with lemon, mackerel with mustard, smoked tuna and all kinds of fishes with Thai, chilli and many other types of dressing. Boneless sardines are an excellent idea for wimps like me (John West). I always like to have a can or two of top-quality tuna for salads – e.g. Ventresca di Tonno, fine belly tuna chunks packed in olive oil from Drago of Sicily (www.natoora.co.uk).

A few words about the sustainability of our canned fish: worldwide, the bluefin and albacore tuna stocks are in danger, so go for tuna-labelled skipjack or yellowfin. If it isn't labelled, I'd avoid it. Canned herring is a good, sustainable and healthy fish, as are canned mackerel fillets. Some canned fishes now carry the Marine Stewardship Council 'blue tick' logo if the fish is sustainable – e.g. Sainsbury's wild Alaskan red salmon.

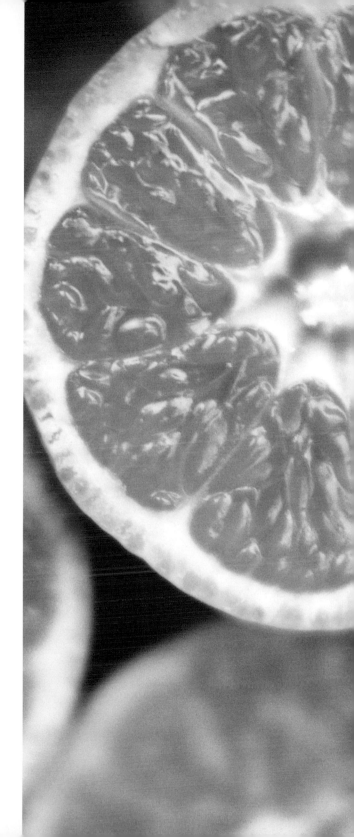

Fruit

Canned fruits, to be frank, don't seem to have come on a long way since the 1960s. You can still buy cans of fruit salad, cling peach slices, pear halves – all in syrup, or unspecified juice. The contents are often just as you remember – pieces of fruit that have lost all their texture, aroma and proper taste. I would rather not bother with most of them. Fruits in jars are not a lot better, by and large.

Just a few are worth stocking for emergency puddings: canned mandarin segments are quite good in a citrus trifle; canned prunes in juice are OK with yogurt and breakfast cereal (and the juice helps keep you regular). Black cherries can be OK. On a slightly different level are Opies fruits – e.g. baby pears with vanilla, and black cherries with kirsch – excellent for quick desserts. And www.theasiancookshop.co.uk or www.spicesofindia.co.uk have some unusual fruits in cans, good for after a spicy meal.

Preserved lemons are, indeed, fruit, though used in savoury Moroccan and other dishes. I like to keep a jar in the cupboard, as they have a special flavour it's hard to replicate any other way (Belazu preserved lemons, www.maroque.co.uk).

Rather than canned fruits, I often prefer to use dried ones, either as they are, if of the ready-to-eat, partial-dried types (but these can be high in sulphur preservatives), or reconstituted by simmering in water or fruit juice. Some of my favourites are dried figs, apricots and plums (prunes), while I am not so keen on dried apples and pears, or cranberries, which have a lot of sugar added to them.

Dried fruits kept too long tend to dry out even more and become unpalatable, especially if you haven't stored them in an airtight tin. Organic dried fruits are sulphur-less and will be a darker colour. www.pulseorganics.com has a good range, as does www.redmoor.net.

Grains

You probably won't have room in your larder to stock more than a few favourites from the dozens of grains (rather than flour or breakfast cereals) now available – and neither will you be able to use them up before they become stale. So choose wisely! Remember, the whole versions contain the most nutrition and dietary fibre, while polished, 'white' varieties contain less of everything except the calories.

Berries of barley, wheat and rye are useful in casseroles and stews. Bulghar wheat is a good whole wheat and quick to cook, so I always have a packet of that in the larder. The supermarkets are not the best place to find the more unusual grains, so look in your local health-food stores and markets, or online. www.goodnessdirect.co.uk has a good choice of whole grains, as well as rice.

Rice is, of course, completely essential – not least because it is one of the least allergenic foods you can find. As the different types of rice are useful for different ethnic dishes, it's hard not to have at least three or four kinds in the cupboard –I always use brown and white basmati, arborio or carnaroli (risotto rice), Spanish paella rice, Thai fragrant rice and red Camargue rice (e.g. Biona), but your choice may be different. www.carluccios.com is good for Italian rices and polenta; www.japanesekitchen.co.uk is good for sushi rice; www.delicioso.co.uk for paella rices; and www.thai-food-online.co.uk for jasmine and sticky rices.

Herbs

While a lot of herbs aren't worth bothering with in dried form, as they lose most of their flavour, aroma and colour, a few – such as rosemary, oregano, thyme and bay leaves – are not too bad, if you use them up within about 3 months. All supermarkets stock a good range, but you can get them for less at www.redmoor.net or www.thebestpossibletaste.co.uk. I would tend not to buy more than 25g at a time of any herb or spice, as you are unlikely to use them up before they go stale. Buy your herbs loose and fill your old jars – no need to waste glass containers every time, and anyway, glass isn't the best container for herbs, which like to be kept in the dark. For opaque herb jars, try www.colloco.co.uk – they do pretty and practical (with a little spoon) ceramic jars.

Jams, marmalades and conserves

This is one area where I am particularly fussy if buying rather than making my own. Virtually all the mass-market jams in our supermarkets contain far too much sugar and not enough fruit – at home the sugar content of my jams is around 45–50 per cent, while the labels on commercial jam will show levels up to 70 per cent!

If you buy at your local Country Market (formerly WI market – www.country-markets.co.uk) you should find preserves made by local women in their own kitchens. This is, of course, no guarantee that they are all terrific cooks, but in my experience the standard of quality is very high. Or the local farmers' markets may yield up some treats. Otherwise, I suggest shopping online for jams, marmalades and conserves which come from various parts of the world. For example, at www.delicioso.co.uk you can buy good Spanish apricot and green fig jam and a great orange marmalade. Carluccio's has a small selection of superb Italian jams – there are branches of his café and shops all over the country (see details on www.carluccios.com). Lovely French conserves, including cherry, framboise, fig and apricot, can be had from www.frenchfoodfreaks.co.uk For a UK jam, try Duchy Originals organic hand-made damson preserve – from www.duchyoriginals.com or Waitrose or Sainsbury's.

Larder accessories

If buying online, my first stop for anything for the larder – from preserving jars, lids and labels, through to storage cans, bottle stoppers and food covers – is www.buy-jam-jars.com It has everything you could ever want and is great to browse.

For hundreds of storage containers, try www.thecookskitchen.com who supply, for example, storage for eggs kept in the larder, and all kinds of clip-lid storage jars for every type of dry food. On the high street (or online at www.johnlewis.com) John Lewis stores have a huge range of kitchen and larder accessories. I find plastic containers with clip-lock lids very useful, as they are ideal for larder, fridge and freezer and are microwaveable – John Lewis have these in many sizes and shapes at very good prices. You'll also find standard sizes at most supermarkets, including Sainsbury's and the Co-op.

If you want something beautiful to store your cakes and biscuits in, you can't do better than the Emma Bridgewater polka-dot range (John Lewis stocks them).

To make extra storage space, you could consider hanging storage racks on the larder or kitchen ceiling or wall. Or make full use of your cupboards by creating extra 'mini shelves' – perhaps tiered; these also make items in a crowded cupboard more easy to see. Lakeland shops (thirty-seven across the country) and online www.lakeland.co.uk have a good, low-cost selection. They also have a huge variety of storage bags, clips and markers, a collection of which is useful for any larder, and longlife storage bags which will help items such as vegetables store for longer without refrigeration.

Meat

There isn't much great meat to be found in cans – although I do have a sneaking regard for a corned beef and pickle sandwich. However, I have tracked down a few items it could be worth stocking. Confit de canard is lovely, tender cooked duck leg portions in a tin (of various sizes), which can be reheated in a frying pan to crisp them up or baked – from www.thegoodfoodnetwork.co.uk. The same company also does authentic cassoulets, including duck, goose and pork, in cans and jars (all these products are made in real confit/cassoulet country in France), and other French casseroles, including coq au vin and a Provençal-style chicken with tomatoes and peppers. www.oilandmore.co.uk also do a French artisan-produced, natural duck, bean and sausage cassoulet in a large jar, and a confit de canard similar to the one above but from a different producer. French cassoulets are best tipped into an ovenproof dish, topped with some breadcrumbs and baked until the crumbs are golden and the stew bubbling.

French chef Guy Simon and his wife Romy set up www.romycuisine.co.uk (07855 531550) from their base in Wales and do several delicious main meals with a one-year shelf-life: for example, Welsh lamb with carrots and garlic, and Welsh Black Beef Bourgignon.

Carluccio's (www.carluccios.com) do two lovely meat pasta sauces – ragu di cinghiale (wild boar) and de lepre (hare). The Look What We Found range contains several all-natural-ingredient meat dishes in longlife pouches – passably good for a quick supper for one (www.lookwhatwefound. co.uk or Sainsbury's and other stores).

See also *Pâtés, terrines and pastes* (page 243).

Miscellaneous

Here are a few items I find useful to stock even though I don't use them all that often: capers (one jar in water, another in sherry vinegar, ideal for chucking into the pan after cooking fish to make a quick pour-over – Delicia, from Sainsbury's); cocoa powder; coconut milk in cans; creamed block coconut; Camp coffee (stronger than ordinary coffee, for cakes, etc.); natural food colourings (used only at Christmas!). All these can be picked up at the supermarket. I do go for good cocoa powder, though, as it makes a difference in baking (I prefer proper chocolate for drinking). Try Divine fairtrade cocoa (www.ecotopia.co.uk and other stores) or The Chocolate Society's drinking chocolate.

Marmite is handy for that moment when you must have a savoury – and you can use it to enrich stews.

A packet of stuffing mix can be used not only for stuffing poultry and pork but also in

sandwiches with cold meats. One of the better dry-stuffing makers is the Shropshire Spice Co., who do a good range (e.g. apricot and almond), including some organic stuffings – buy from www. shropshire-spice.co.uk and Waitrose.

I also include stock in here. While it would be wonderful always to make our own stock, it is something I make from scratch only occasionally, so good-quality stock base is essential. If stock cubes are good enough for Marco Pierre, they are good enough for me! For vegetable soups and similar, I use Marigold low-salt bouillon in a cardboard pot; otherwise I use Kallo low-salt vegetable stock cubes and also their organic chicken and beef cubes. Most stock cubes (other than those labelled low salt) are very salty, so if you use them don't add much extra salt to soups, casseroles, etc.). For French casseroles and other dishes try More Than Gourmet real reduced stocks in a pot (www.goodfoodnetwork.co.uk).

Nuts and seeds

Nuts and seeds are extremely handy storecupboard items in their many guises: raw in the shell; raw shelled; raw shelled chopped or flaked; raw shelled ground; whole roasted or toasted; roasted salted; speciality (e.g. cocktail nuts, gifts); butters and, of course, pastes; and confectionery such as marzipan.

Fresh raw shell-on nuts will last a few weeks in a cool, dry, dark larder, but not indefinitely. Kept in a warm place they may well go rancid. Buy them from the shops when in season – for UK nuts such as hazelnuts and walnuts, that will be autumn.

Raw shelled nuts also don't last for ever; in fact, they last for a shorter time than those in the shell, which offers some protection (old nuts and seeds may taste 'off' and their healthy fats may

have oxygenated so that they are no longer good for you), so don't buy in large bags unless you know you will use them within weeks. Also try to buy them from a shop where you know turnover is high, so that they haven't been hanging around the shelves for months (supermarkets will be good on this score, while nuts and seeds sold loose from small local health-food shops and delis may fail the freshness test).

Raw shelled nuts which have been chopped, flaked or ground last even less time – once the nut is cut its vital oils begin to break down. It is preferable to buy whole nuts and chop or grind them yourself as you want them.

The fresh nuts that I find most useful and desirable are walnuts because of their strong and distinctive taste; almonds as they are used in so many savoury and sweet dishes; Brazils because they are very high in magnesium and selenium, two important minerals which can easily be lacking in our diets; cashews, great for Asian dishes; hazelnuts for muesli; and pistachios and macadamias for cocktail nuts. I couldn't live without pine nuts – a great source of minerals too – because I love Mediterranean cooking, and some mixed seeds for home-made muesli.

Fresh nuts and seeds are so widely available it is not worth giving you many stockists, but, as those small packets of nuts in the supermarkets are so expensive, if you can get together with three or four neighbours or local friends it would be worth ordering larder quantities from www.pulseorganics.com and dividing them between you. Even after postage costs, their organic, ethical nuts work out much lower in cost than those in most supermarkets. Or try www.countryproducts.co.uk.

Roasted or toasted nuts have lost some of their essential oils in the heating and cooking process, so try to toast nuts yourself if you really need them, and do just a minimal, light-golden toasting. Salted roast nuts are high in salt, so why not try other cocktail varieties – for example, Country Products do chilli-coated peanuts and also roasted but unsalted peanuts. www.delicioso.co.uk do toasted, sugared Spanish almonds, or a less expensive option is honey-roasted cashews or rosemary-infused roasted mixed nuts (Waitrose). Yogurt-coated nuts are very sweet, not as healthy as they sound, while dark-chocolate-coated nuts can be very good indeed (try Divine Dark Chocolate Coated Brazil Nuts, www.ukorganics.co.uk).

For muesli-making you may like to buy nut mixes, or even trail mix, combining nuts, seeds, dried fruit, coconut flakes, etc. – widely available.

Nut butters are very useful for toppings for bread and toast, to add protein to vegetarian dishes. Mass-market peanut butter contains sugar, but Suma organic peanut butters don't (www.ethicalsuperstore.com and independent stores) and some are free from salt as well. You can buy Crazy Jack organic marzipan from www.goodnessdirect.co.uk and major supermarkets.

Oils

While every supermarket stocks a good range of olive oils and some other oils (for a rundown, see page 68), if you are an 'oil buff' – or would like to be – then you may be better off visiting more specialist shops, or stores which have a dedicated oil counter. Oil & Vinegar shops, of which there are ten or so across the UK, are a great starting point if you're near one (check at www.oilvinegar.com), as you can taste the oils and they are decanted for you as you watch. They also do lots of other ingredients that complement oils.

Graig Farm (www.graigfarm.co.uk) does a selection of organic, artisan, cold-pressed oils from different plants, including rapeseed, olive, walnut and Brazil, at reasonable prices. Fortnum & Mason do several high-end single-estate olive oils (www.fortnumandmason.com) and www.oilandmore.co.uk has an excellent range of all kinds of gourmet oils.

For more choice of oils from individual countries, try www.delicioso.co.uk for Spanish oils and a good range of flavoured oils; for Italian oil try the Italian Olive Oil Company (www.oliveoil4u.co.uk) who have plenty of detailed information on their products on the site. For French, try www.frenchflavour.co.uk (they also do a good range of flavoured oils, including truffle oil, lemon oil and spice oil) and for Greek try www.thegoodfoodnetwork.co.uk

Of course if you live in a city or large town you should have nearby a range of ethnic delis and groceries which will undoubtedly have an oil section worth browsing.

For oils other than olive oil, try www.getoily.com – horrid name, but they do a great range of oils, from argan oil through almond and hazelnut to avocado and even pine nut oil.

Pasta and noodles

I keep a small selection, including spaghetti, linguine, shells, lasagne sheets, penne and small soup pasta, which seems to cover most eventualities.

Basic dried durum wheat pasta from the supermarket can be fine – especially if you pay a little bit more for the Italian-produced brands. De Cecco is a good Italian brand, available at Sainsbury's. If you go to Italian shops you will find what is probably better-than-average-quality pasta – e.g. www.carluccios.com and stores nationwide. There are some nice, slow-dried Tuscan pastas at www.findfoodstore.co.uk including organic ones, and at www.natoora.co.uk where you will also find organic and regional Italian pastas.

Bronze pasta (e.g. Napolina, Biona) is extruded through bronze dye to create a rough and porous finish which holds the sauce really well.

Most dried pastas contain just wheat, but some do contain eggs (e.g. Barilla Egg Pasta) – check the label if you want to avoid eggs. Wholewheat pasta contains more fibre and sometimes takes a little longer to cook. It isn't authentically Italian.

'Quick-cook' pasta will cook from dry in about 5 minutes, but I find it is hardly worth it for the time you save as you do lose some flavour and texture. Microwave pasta is basically pre-cooked pasta in a longlife pouch which you just reheat in the microwave for 2 minutes. I would regard it as a standby, as the better-textured dried pasta can cook in only 10 minutes, or even less for fine types such as spaghettini.

You can buy a few ranges of longlife filled pastas and gnocchi (usually in transparent, shrink-wrapped packs or controlled atmosphere pouches) from all the supermarkets; these may be OK as a standby for a hungry teen, but I can't vouch for them.

I tend to stock just medium egg-thread noodles and rice noodles, but all noodles are quick to prepare and so if you are a great noodle fan you might like to expand your range to include Japanese soba (buckwheat) noodles, Thai Pad Noodles and fine egg-thread. All the supermarkets stock most of these. For more unusual noodles, www.thai-food-online.co.uk stock a variety, including triangular rice flake noodles. Japanese udon, ramen and somen noodles are available at the Japanese Kitchen (www.japanesekitchen.co.uk).

Pâtés, terrines and pastes

Happily I have found several decent fish and seafood pâtés that you can store in the larder. www.dukeshillham.co.uk has a longlife Coquille St-Jacques (scallop) terrine which is delicious – as good as a fresh seafood pâté – and they also do a crayfish pâté, and meat (e.g. wild boar), duck and quail terrines. www.britnett-carver.co.uk do rillettes de saumon fumé and a brandade of salt cod (as well as some good meat terrines). And the French Pantry of Ludlow (www.thefrenchpantry.co.uk) has two artisan-made fish pâtés – smoked trout, and salmon terrine with sorrel.

Superb meat terrines are available from www.romycuisine.co.uk (all free range with a one-year shelf-life but no artificial additives). www.oilandmore.co.uk has terrines from France, including coarse rillettes de canard and terrine de canard. www.thegoodfoodnetwork.co.uk also does a range of authentic terrines from France, including guinea fowl, hare, and chicken liver pâté, all at good prices. You can buy olive paste (tapenade) from the same company and also from Natoora, where you can get a superb artichoke paste from Sole e Natura, which is lovely on toast or crostini (www.natoora.co.uk).

Anchoide is an anchovy paste usually made with olive oil, garlic, lemon and herbs – and sometimes capers and maybe tomato or olives – which is a good standby for toast or beating into mayonnaise as a dip, or thinned a little and used as a pasta sauce. Good delis will stock a version, or try www.confitdirect.co.uk – they also do lovely aubergine and courgette pâtés. Find good Italian pastes (e.g. for topping toast, crostini, bruschetta) at www.carluccios.com and at www.graigfarm.co.uk – their organic Pugliese tomatoey-spread is delicious.

Pulses

A few bags of dried pulses are a good idea on the grounds of cost and on saving storage space (the dried beans take up less space than cooked cans), and sometimes on grounds of taste and texture – but on convenience they are slightly less attractive than cans as most take more faffing about: soaking, pre-boiling and then long simmering.

Therefore the quick-cook dried pulses win all round: all kinds of lentils, brown, green Puy, black, even the refined red ones, are perfect storecupboard items for soups, stews, purées, as a vegetable instead of potatoes (and much higher in protein). Merchant Gourmet do a very good Puy lentil (most supermarkets) but the un-named ones from your local health-food shop should be fine. Check for tiny stones before using.

Split peas also cook quickly and can be used in a similar way but are much softer and sweeter.

Of the other dried pulses, if there is one type that you use a lot – in my case cannellini beans and borlotti beans – then it is worth stocking some and making the effort to plan ahead to cook them. www.thespicewarehouse.com has a good range of dried pulses should you want to order online.

Canned pulses are now ubiquitous in the shops, so there is little point searching for them on the internet unless you are after something very unusual.

Decent baked beans in tomato sauce are worth seeking out – I love B&M Original Baked Beans (www.americansweets.co.uk), but that said, the very cheap beans at Aldi (about 22 pence a can as I write) are incredibly good.

You can also get canned speciality pulse items – for example, Puy Lentil Sauce in goose fat (www.thegoodfoodnetwork.co.uk) to heat and serve with duck. And of course there are spicy pre-prepared pulse purées – try curried lentil moong or chana dhal mughlai from www.spicesofindia.co.uk as a quick meal on their own or as an accompaniment to a vegetable curry.

Salad dressings and mayonnaise

If you have some decent oils and vinegars, mustard, sugar and seasonings in the cupboard then you don't really need to buy ready-made salad dressings. Most of them are not, in truth, very nice and often have a long, long list of artificial-sounding ingredients. But for emergencies, there are one or two exceptions.

Pizza Express Balsamic Dressing has an impressively short list of ingredients and a good authentic balance of olive oil and vinegar (Tesco). Tesco's own Organic French Dressing isn't too bad at all, and Newman's Own Balsamic is OK. The Mary Berry range of dressings, including Caesar and various others as well as basic salad dressing, are free from artificial flavours and preservatives and contain good-quality ingredients.

A jar of ready mayonnaise is a handy item – none of them matches the real thing, but if you think of them as entities in their own right and forget all about home-made mayo while you are eating them, one or two are fine. Simply Delicious organic mayonnaise is nice and light and lemony, and perhaps my favourite of the mainstream varieties. Egg-free Granovita Mayola may be useful to know about for people with an egg allergy: from www.pulseorganics.com.

Many people love salad cream for its vinegary tang. If you do, then Heinz Salad Cream is still the best. There is a nice organic salad cream by Meridian sold at Pulse (www.pulseorganics.com) and health-food stores.

Salt

Although the chemical composition of salt is virtually the same whether it is basic table salt or the most expensive organic sea salt crystals, it is nice to have a salt that looks good and is preferably local – or at least not from thousands of miles away – when you're cooking.

Anglesey Sea Salt is Soil Association-certified organic, from www.dukeshillham.co.uk. Sel de Guérande is high-quality French coarse-grained sea salt from www.thegoodfoodnetwork.co.uk – ideal for grinders. Maldon sea salt is a good brand with flakes (for cooking) and crystals too and is widely available. Cornish Sea Salt claims to contain over sixty trace elements and has 'more taste for less salt' – from www.localfoodshop.co.uk, Fortnum & Mason, Selfridge's Food Hall and independents nationwide (0845 337 5277).

Savoury snacks

If you don't want nuts, a couple of healthy alternatives are broad beans – habas fritas, roasted broad beans from Spain. Get them plain roasted or with a crunchy spicy coating from www.olivesetal.co.uk or delis nationwide. Olivesetal also do chilli rice puffs.

Tyrrells (www.tyrrellspotatochips.co.uk) do good mixed root vegetable chips (a mix of carrot, beetroot and parsnip) and they also do habas fritas, from stores nationwide, and three dips to dip your chips into.

Soup

Ready-made soup for the larder is notoriously not delicious and I would normally recommend, as it is so easy to do, that you whizz up your own in the kitchen. But a few brands are worth considering for lazy or busy lunchtimes or unexpected guests.

www.dukeshillham.co.uk sells real French fish soup in a bottle and so do www.thegoodfoodnetwork.co.uk and www.confitdirect.co.uk and Waitrose (all Perard brand). If you have any cream, adding a dash makes them even better. Seeds of Change make an edible range of organic soups in longlife foil pouches with no artificial ingredients (widely available).

Spices

Dried spices are almost as good as fresh, by and large, so you can stock the cupboard with abandon. It is best to buy them whole if you can, as they keep better and retain flavour and aroma, but ground spices will last for a couple of months in a cool, dark, dry place in airtight jars.

You can also buy spices preserved in oil – e.g. garlic, chillies, ginger – and ready mashed or chopped.

Try to expand your range rather than just sticking to a few tried and tested ones such as cumin, coriander and chilli. Fenugreek, mace, star anise and many more can add excitement to your cooking.

Spice blends are becoming more and more popular. Each country has its own blends, so ethnic websites and local ethnic delis are a good source of these, but www.thebestpossibletaste.co.uk has a really good selection. www.spicesofindia.co.uk is another good online store and there is a good selection at www.spiceworld.uk.com – buy loose or in jars. And spice pastes are essential, too – see *Cooking pastes*, page 234.

Store your spices in opaque (ceramic or stainless-steel) jars, which you can buy from kitchen stores such as www.thecookskitchen.com or spice shops such as www.spicewarehouse.com.

Sugar, honey and sweeteners

While all types of sugar have almost the same nutritional profile (brown has only small traces of minerals), there is no doubt that a decent cane sugar tastes nicer than a highly refined, mass-produced beet one. There are times, though, when the latter is acceptable – white icing for cakes, in some drinks (such as, for example, home-made lemonade, when tastier sugars can spoil or corrupt the flavour of the drink), in jams when dark cane sugars would spoil, and so on.

A good sugar makes the most difference to baking, desserts, puddings and confectionery, and if you do a lot of sweet cooking you will find that having a range of different grades of sugar in the larder will be a boon. The brown sugars can add moisture and colour as well as flavour to cakes and biscuits, so I would say a basic range for baking would include a light soft brown Muscovado, a dark soft brown Muscovado, and some treacle. Brown fine-grain (caster) sugar is good for easy dissolving and sauces, while demerara is good for coffee and preserving sugar is necessary if you make your own jam. Most types of sugar are available as organic.

Most supermarkets now have a very good range of sugars to choose from. Most stock Billington's, all of whose sugars are good-quality, unrefined cane – their very dark molasses sugar is lovely in rich fruit cakes and a little added to a marinade or savoury sauce can make a difference to the flavour. They even do an unrefined icing sugar, which will give a nice honey colour to your icing.

You may find more organic and specialist varieties at delis and health-food stores. Or try www.goodnessdirect.com for a range of organic and fairtrade cane sugars. This company stocks a huge range of natural sweeteners, too – from organic agave syrup to brown rice syrup and maple syrup.

You can use honey or syrup instead of sugar for sweetening many dishes and sometimes in baking. For baking, a standard blended honey is fine, but for toast and drizzling, a single-blossom honey is preferable for flavour. Goodness Direct stocks dozens of honeys from across the world, but if you prefer more local produce then try your nearest farmers' market or Country Market, or your local health-food store. For European honeys, www.delicioso.co.uk has a nice range of Spanish honeys, while www.wallysdeli.co.uk sells Greek and Welsh honeys and www.frenchflavour.co.uk does several good French ones. www.brynderihoneyfarm.com sells its own Welsh honey and a range of flavoured honey spreads for bread.

Table sauces and condiments

For the table, a few bottles of something tasty to perk up cold meats, cheese, pâtés, and so on are obligatory.

The iconic brands can be fine – Lea & Perrins Worcestershire sauce being one example, and Heinz Tomato Ketchup another. But these days there are plenty more good sauces to choose from. L & P themselves have made a thicker sauce called Lea & Perrins Tomato and Worcester Table Sauce (Tesco) which I love with Sunday cooked breakfast.

Reggae Reggae Jerk Barbecue Sauce is delicious, with a nice, natural list of ingredients (Tesco and other stores). Sarsons Worcester sauce contains no anchovies and is suitable for vegetarians, unlike the Lea & Perrins version. Also don't forget a good horseradish – it's hard to get a decent one, but Simply Delicious organic horseradish sauce is very nice if you don't want it too strong, while Gloucestershire-based www.kitchengardenpreserves.co.uk do a nice hand-made, all-natural one. They also do a lovely range of mustards, cranberry and other jellies, and several organic products.

www.formanandfield.com have a good choice of luxury bottled sauces. A few sweet sauces are also handy. Try Rowse Signature Dark Belgian Chocolate Sauce, English Provender Co's Very Lazy Belgian Chocolate Sauce (Booths, Tesco) or www.lakeland.co.uk do a good chocolate sauce called East of Boston; Best of Taste summer-fruit coulis (and other varieties, all good from www.realfooddirect.co.uk). I have just discovered Tesco Finest Ginger Dessert Sauce for vanilla ice cream or pancakes – it is really nice.

Tomatoes

As tomatoes are such an important storecupboard fruit/vegetable, they get a listing of their own. I certainly couldn't manage without them in my cupboards.

Here's what I consider essential: canned whole Italian tomatoes; canned chopped Italian tomatoes; passata (either in jars or longlife Tetra Packs); tomato purée or paste (tubes are handiest); sundried tomato paste in little jars; sundried tomatoes in oil (I think they are nicer than those just dried in packs). All these can be found in all the

supermarkets and price is not necessarily an indication of quality – Aldi's canned tomatoes are superb and only about 25 pence a can, for example.

You can also find tomatoey items which, while not essential, can add depth and pleasure to your meals. Terre à terre home-made smoked sundried tomatoes with herbs and spices are good chopped into a tomato dressing for grilled pork or chicken (www.terreaterre.co.uk). www.goodnessdirect.co.uk do organic cherry tomatoes in a can. You can also buy variations of chopped tomatoes – with chilli, with herbs, with basil, for example, and Waitrose do a nice one with garlic and oil, and another with sliced olives, which can all be handy for speeding up the making of a pasta tomato sauce (www.waitrosedeliver.com). Heinz Tomato Frito is passata with added garlic and seasonings.

Vegetables

Canned: There are not many tinned vegetables that I buy because, as with tinned fruit, the quality of taste, texture and appearance is often poor. But a few things do translate quite well to the can, so my shortlist is artichokes (canned in water) – dry them well and use them in antipasto, in sauces or soup; celery hearts (no good for salad but fine for soups and casseroles); ratatouille (good brands include Waitrose own brand) – jazz it up with some fresh herbs or chopped chilli if you have any; red peppers – fine for slicing into sauces and soups; mushy peas (Harry Ramsden's) are OK with fish and chips – add some garlic and serve with grilled sausages; Eazy fried onions are handy in emergencies (Tesco, Asda and most supermarkets).

Jars: I like to keep a couple of jars of vegetables in oil – artichokes are good, as are mixed mushrooms, grilled aubergines and courgettes. I also have a jar of Opies pickled onions in balsamic vinegar (Sainsbury's).

Dried: If you count mushrooms as vegetables, they dry very successfully and I always have a small packet or two of mixed wild mushrooms and one or two other varieties – shiitake for Chinese meals and porcini for Italian sauces. Most supermarkets stock at least one or two types, but Lidl usually have a good range in stock at a good price, or you can find a good selection at www.smithymushrooms.co.uk, including girolles and morels.

Merchant Gourmet does a good range of sundried vegetables including aubergines and sweet peppers – you can buy online at www.merchant-gourmet.com.

www.spiceworld.uk.com has a small selection of other types of dried vegetable, including carrot flakes and bell peppers, which could be handy for adding to casseroles and soups.

Purées: Libby's pure pumpkin purée comes in a can, good for a quick dessert or in baking and even added to milk for a smoothie (www.americansweets.co.uk). Gia Vegetable Purée in a tube is a good addition to stews and sauces (Booths, Morrisons).

Speciality: Infinity Stuffed Vine Leaves (from www.pulseorganics.com) are quite good as an instant starter – drizzle over some lemon oil. www.theasiancookshop.co.uk has lots of Asian and oriental vegetables in cans. Or try www.spicesofindia.com for vegetables such as aubergines in tomato sauce or gaigan bharta – mashed aubergines with ginger and chillies. Lovely!

Vinegars

You can go on and on with vinegars – raspberry vinegar, tarragon vinegar, distilled vinegar, light vinegar, white balsamic vinegar, fig and balsamic vinegar – but you probably won't have room to stock more than five or six. My own larder has red and white wine vinegars, two balsamics – one extremely good and the other more standard – sherry vinegar, cider vinegar, rice vinegar, and sometimes it has pickling (white) vinegar.

Most supermarkets stock the basics, but if you want a top-notch wine or balsamic vinegar you may have to look a bit harder. Fattorie Giacobazzi aged balsamics always get well reviewed, as do Belazu.

If you want to push out the boat, buy Giuseppe Giusti vintage balsamics (their basic balsamic is around £12.50 for 25cl, but some go up to £100) – they claim to be the oldest producers of balsamic vinegar in Modena. Enquire for stockists at www.giusti.it or go to www.londonfinewine.co.uk.

www.carluccios.com do a really good aged balsamic at £18.95 for 25cl. Or a good idea is to go for a tasting pack – Carluccio's have a four-pack of 10ml each for £12.95.

Find rice vinegar, great for Asian cooking, at www.theasiancookshop.co.uk and some supermarkets.

www.oilandmore.co.uk have a very good selection of all kinds of top-quality vinegars, including Banyuls red wine vinegar, or at £82 for 100ml (as I write) – a forty-year-old balsamic vinegar from La Vecchia Dispensa.

Look for vinegars with a 6 per cent acid level.

www.goodnessdirect.co.uk has a good selection of organic vinegars.

Index